The Wind and Wind-Chorus Music of Anton Bruckner

Recent Titles in
Contributions to the Study of Music and Dance

Whose Master's Voice?: The Development of Popular Music in
Thirteen Cultures
Alison J. Ewbank and Fouli T. Papageorgiou, editors

The Piece as a Whole: Studies in Holistic Musical Analysis
Hugh Aitken

Mythology as Metaphor: Romantic Irony, Critical Theory, and Wagner's *Ring*
Mary A. Cicora

Wagner's *Ring* and German Drama: Comparative Studies in Mythology and History in
Drama
Mary A. Cicora

Tchaikovsky and His Contemporaries: A Centennial Symposium
Alexandar Mihailovic, editor

Chopin Through His Contemporaries: Friends, Lovers, and Rivals
Pierre Azoury

Otto Laske: Navigating New Musical Horizons
Jerry Tabor, editor

Perspectives on the Grateful Dead: Critical Writings
Robert G. Weiner, editor

The Cultivation of Body and Mind in Nineteenth-Century American Delsartism
Nancy Lee Chalfa Ruyter

Domenico Cimarosa: His Life and His Operas
Nick Rossi and Talmage Fauntleroy

The Writings and Letters of Konrad Wolff
Ruth Gillen, editor

Nomai Dance Drama: A Surviving Spirit of Medieval Japan
Susan M. Asai

The Wind and Wind-Chorus Music of Anton Bruckner

Keith William Kinder

Contributions to the Study of Music and Dance, Number 51

Greenwood Press
Westport, Connecticut • London

Library of Congress Cataloging-in-Publication Data

Kinder, Keith William.
    The wind and wind-chorus music of Anton Bruckner / by Keith
William Kinder.
        p.   cm.—(Contributions to the study of music and dance,
ISSN 0193–9041 ; no. 51)
    A study of the composer's use of wind instruments in non-
orchestral contexts, chiefly in vocal works employing accompanying
wind instruments.
    Includes bibliographical references and index.
    ISBN 0–313–30834–9 (alk. paper)
    1. Bruckner, Anton, 1824–1896—Criticism and interpretation.
2. Bruckner, Anton, 1824–1896—Contributions in instrumentation and
orchestration.   3. Instrumentation and orchestration.   I. Title.
II. Series.
ML410.B88K43   2000
780′.92—dc21   98–23935

British Library Cataloguing in Publication Data is available.

Library of Congress Catalog Card Number: 98–23935
ISBN: 0–313–30834–9
ISSN: 0193–9041

First published in 2000

Greenwood Press, 88 Post Road West, Westport, CT 06881
An imprint of Greenwood Publishing Group, Inc.
www.greenwood.com

Printed in the United States of America

The paper used in this book complies with the
Permanent Paper Standard issued by the National
Information Standards Organization (Z39.48–1984).

10 9 8 7 6 5 4 3 2 1

Copyright Acknowledgment

The author and publisher gratefully acknowledge permission from Albany Records and John
Proffitt to include excerpts from the Disc Jacket Notes for *Choral Works of Anton Bruckner* (1991),
Albany Records CD, Troy 063.

Contents

ACKNOWLEDGMENTS   vii

INTRODUCTION   ix

1: THE FIRST SMALL STEPS OF A MASTER 1841–45   1

2: ST. FLORIAN 1845–55   7

3: LINZ I: THE SECHTER HIATUS 1856–61   35

4: LINZ II: "A WATCHDOG UNCHAINED" 1861–68   39

5: THE *E-MINOR MASS—WAB 27*   71

6: VIENNA: "A TONAL ANTI-CHRIST" 1868–96   101

7: STRIDING INTO ETERNITY   125

APPENDIX A: THE *APOLLO-MARSCH— WAB 115*   131

APPENDIX B: *LITANEI—WAB 132*   133

APPENDIX C: SOURCES   135

BIBLIOGRAPHY   137

INDEX   141

Acknowledgments

The author gratefully acknowledges the assistance of the following individuals and institutions: Bruckner Society of America, and Dr. Charles Eble; Internationale Bruckner-Gesellschaft, Vienna, and Dr. Andrea Harrandt; Österreichische National-bibliothek, Vienna; the music libraries of the University of Iowa, University of Colorado, University of Washington, Michigan State University, University of Toronto, University of Western Ontario, McMaster University; Mr. Werner Probst, Meckenheim; my translator, Ms. Ruth Thomas; and especially my wife, Susan Smith, for her careful editing of the manuscript, her encouragement, and her love.

Introduction

Musically, there are two Anton Bruckners. The life of this major nineteenth-century Austrian musician is bisected into two almost equal parts by a change of compositional style so dramatic and so total that it is unprecedented among major composers.[1] Had Bruckner not undergone this stylistic metamorphosis in the early 1860s, he would be remembered today as an excellent organist and a highly skilled church musician who composed a substantial amount of competent but undistinguished music. Few of his compositions would ever be performed. The musical repertoire would be without the eleven magnificent symphonies upon which much of his reputation rests today. Throughout the first half of his life, Bruckner immersed himself in a relentless quest to learn everything that could be taught to him about traditional musical principles—form, harmony, counterpoint, orchestration. During the last half of his life, he travelled on a harmonic journey that left tradition far behind, and ultimately took him to the fringes of nineteenth-century tonality.

Bruckner scholars have concentrated their efforts on the post-1860 works, which are, quite rightly, seen as the composer's major contribution to the musical literature. However, closer inspection of the early works, including those that employ wind instruments, reveals that many of the landmarks of his style were present from the very beginning. Many of these compositions illustrate a daring harmonic imagination, an ability to construct dramatic and expressive melodies, substantial contrapuntal invention, and, at least in the cases of the *Requiem* of 1848–49 and the *Missa solemnis* of 1854, an ability to conceive and realize large-scale works. While few of them approach the individuality or innovation that mark the later works, many are far more interesting than has generally been acknowledged.

---

[1] The career of American composer George Rochberg in our own century might rival this contention.

Bruckner's works using wind instruments in non orchestral contexts appeared throughout his entire career, and vary widely in scope, scoring, and intent. They incorporate the best aspects of both of his styles, and, to a large degree, reflect the progress of his professional life. The earliest compositions are small-scale, as was dictated by the limited musical means at his disposal. As his situation improved, his wind works grew in breadth and complexity so that the latest pieces provide significant analytical challenges. Most of these works are liturgical in intent, and demonstrate a profound understanding of Roman Catholic doctrine. On the other hand, this repertoire includes several outstanding secular compositions that deserve much broader acknowledgment than they have been assigned thus far. Bruckner's contribution to the wind literature is substantial and important. The purpose of this study is to bring to his contribution the recognition it so richly deserves.

From the perspective of more than a century, it is difficult to imagine that until his thirty-first year, Anton Bruckner prepared himself for a career as a school teacher, not as a musician. His father (also Anton Bruckner) was the schoolmaster in the upper Austrian village of Ansfelden (Cooke/Nowak 1980, 352). When Anton Jr. was born in 1824, the elder Bruckner assumed that the boy would follow in his footsteps, and soon began laying the groundwork for his son's career. Since school-masters in Austrian villages were expected to assume responsibility for music in the church (Watson 1977, 6), this early training included a substantial amount of musical instruction. By age ten the young Bruckner was able to substitute for his father at the organ during church services (Cooke/Nowak 1980, 352).

Anton Bruckner Sr. recognized and encouraged his son's consuming interest in music, and quickly realized that he needed instruction beyond what was available in Ansfelden. Consequently, in the spring of 1835, the boy was sent to study with his godfather, Johann Baptist Weiss,[2] the schoolmaster and organist in Hörsching, a small town near Linz. Bruckner lived in Hörsching for approximately eighteen months, receiving his first formal instruction in organ playing and attempting his first compositions. Throughout his life he frequently expressed his gratitude to Weiss and remembered these days with fondness.

In December 1836 Bruckner was summoned back to Ansfelden. His father was seriously ill, and the young man was needed to deputize in the schoolhouse and the church (Cooke/Nowak 1980, 353). Six months later, in June 1837, Anton Bruckner Sr. died of consumption (Watson 1977, 4).

Faced with the dissolution of her household, Bruckner's mother proved herself to be far-sighted and resourceful. Refusing to allow her eldest child to forgo his education because of the death of her husband, she appealed to Michael Arneth, the

---

[2]"Cousin Weiss" was an accomplished musician who composed a number of sacred works, including a *Requiem* in E-flat major published by Lanninger in 1892. In 1850, some years after Bruckner's tuition had abruptly ended, Weiss was duped into accepting responsibility for a church fund from which a large sum had been embezzled. When the police arrived to question him, he fled into the graveyard and committed suicide (Watson 1977, 4, 10–11).

prior of the monastery at nearby St. Florian, asking that the boy be accepted into the abbey's choir school (Cooke/Nowak 1980, 353). Arneth was interested in music and made a place at St. Florian for the young man. Bruckner lived at the abbey until 1840, studying music until his voice broke, then deciding to prepare for a career in teaching. By the summer of 1841, he had completed the basic teacher training course and was a qualified assistant teacher (Watson 1977, 139).

Bruckner's initial years at St. Florian had an enormous impact on the rest of his life. For the first time he received instruction in educational basics—reading, writing, arithmetic—and had lessons on organ, violin, and in musical theory. However, perhaps the most lasting impact was in areas that had little to do with music or education. The great Baroque monastery with its magnificent organ be-came his spiritual home—a home to which he returned again and again for solace and spiritual refreshment. He also gained a powerful ally in Michael Arneth. Arneth had apparently recognized Bruckner's musical talents, and saw to it that he received appointments that permitted both his education and his career to develop.

Chapter 1

The First Small Steps of a Master 1841–45

In October 1841 Anton Bruckner was assigned to the position of assistant school-master in Windhaag, a small town near the Bohemian border (Watson 1977, 7). As assistant, the young man was in complete servitude to his superior, Franz Fuchs. In addition to his duties in the schoolhouse and the church, he was saddled with a multitude of menial tasks that included ringing the morning bell at 4:00 A.M., the evening bell at 9:00 P.M., and working in his supervisor's fields. Eventually Bruck-ner refused to accept such lowly assignments, and Fuchs complained to St. Florian (Doernberg 1960, 33). When Arneth arrived for an inspection, the schoolmaster expressed his displeasure with Bruckner and apparently was particularly upset by his preoccupation with music (Watson 1977, 7–8). Bruckner was promptly trans-ferred to the even smaller village of Kronstorf.

While ostensibly a punishment, this transfer proved that Arneth was indeed looking out for Bruckner's best interests. Kronstorf was situated between the cul-turally active towns of Steyr and Enns, and was within walking distance of St. Florian. Bruckner arrived in January 1843 and quickly established relationships in all four communities that permitted the continuous development of his musical education. He was, however, still preparing for a career in teaching, not in music, and to this end he passed the final exam for assistant teachers in May 1845 (Watson 1977, 9). He was now ready to accept the much better position that was about to present itself.

Bruckner's compositions[1] from these formative years consist of small-scale liturgical works, organ pieces, and a few unaccompanied male choruses. Most are undistinguished and derivative, drawing heavily on the music he was studying at the

---

[1]Most of the earliest pieces are, in fact, composition exercises. The four organ preludes of 1837 display the usual awkward voice leading of many first compositions, but they also have some remarkable enharmonic modulations that are clear portents of the future.

time. One work of this period employs wind instruments and therefore is of particular interest to this study.

CHORALMESSE IN C-DUR (WINDHAAGER)—WAB 25

Bruckner's first Mass was written at Windhaag, probably sometime during 1842 (Schulze 1986, 3). The musical resources of the village were limited, so the work was conceived on a small scale and in a simple style. Scored for solo alto, two horns, and organ, it employs a text compressed to the absolute minimum and is exclusively homophonic in texture.[2] It was written for Maria Jobst, daughter of a local resident, and the alto soloist in the church choir (Göllerich/Auer 1974, I: 170). Bruckner's designation of his composition as a "Chorale Mass" referred to its simple, hymnlike style and did not imply the use of specific liturgical melodies.[3] Such masses were frequently performed in country churches, especially during Advent and Lent (Schulze 1986, 3).

Tonally this work follows conventional harmonic patterns, but, as Bruckner was to do throughout his life, it also contains frequent modulations (often to rather distant keys) without the use of pivot chords. For example, in the *Kyrie* the opening phrase establishes the tonic—C major—but the subsequent phrase modulates very abruptly to A-flat major. Similar unprepared changes of key occur in all movements. The manuscript consists of a set of parts without a full score. For the most part, the organ music is sparingly figured (Schulze 1986, 3) allowing for considerable variety in its realization.[4] At bar 15 of the *Kyrie*, Bruckner specifies the necessary realization, which produces an interesting juxtaposition of C minor and C major.

Example 1.1:
Windhaager Mass—Kyrie—bars 15–16

Elisabeth Maier has connected the opening phrase of the *Kyrie* to the plainchant *Kyrie Deus sempiterne* (Maier 1988, 119), and while the relationship is

---

[2]This work is apparently an Austrian *Landmesse* or *missa brevis*. In such pieces the text, particularly the *Credo*, was abbreviated in order to shorten the duration of the work as a whole (Redlich 1955, 66).

[3]It is, however, important to observe that plainchant influenced much of the melodic construction.

[4]The lack of specifics regarding the figuration accounts for the considerable differences in the realization of this score in its first publication—Göllerich/Auer 1974, I: 173–89—and the recent performing edition published by Carus-Verlag.

not exact, it is clearly audible.

Example 1.2A:
Windhaager Mass—Kyrie—bars 1–4

Example 1.2B:
Kyrie Deus sempiterne—Liber Usualis—p. 22

In the *Gloria* the nineteenth-century principle of third relationships is much in evidence. The first two phrases cadence on an E major chord, the third reestablishes the tonic, C major, then subsequent phrases explore A minor, F major, and D minor. The concluding section of the movement returns to the tonic via A minor and F major. This emphasis on third relationships is surprising, since Bruckner's musical education had focused on pre-nineteenth-century models. This movement also incorporates a number of descending octave skips in the melodic line. Such melodic construction became a Bruckner fingerprint in ensuing years.[5]

The *Credo*, like the *Gloria*, employs only a portion of the extensive text usually associated with these sections of the Mass. It also continues the emphasis on harmonic third relationships. Many writers have noted that the opening and closing phrases of this movement are based on the Gregorian *Credo in unum Deum*. Bruckner's use of this well-known plainchant comes as no surprise considering that his familiarity with the Roman Catholic liturgy was grounded in active involvement with church music from a very early age.

Example 1.3A:
Liber Usualis—Credo I, II, IV

---

[5]Another interesting detail about this movement was noted by Leopold Nowak. At measures 49–50, the words "*Cum Sancto Spiritu*" are set to the unison motive, *doh-sol-lah-mi*, which Wagner was to employ as the "bell motive" in *Parsifal* some years later (Nowak 1988, 88–89). Manfred Wagner sees the appearance of this motive as a deliberate poetic gesture on Bruckner's part—a church bell calling down or announcing the arrival on earth of the Holy Spirit (Wagner 1996, 23). Interestingly, the same motive, also in unison, appears at bars 40–41 of the *Credo* (Gruber 1988, 132). Since the words are "*Et resurrexit tertia ...*," it would appear that another poetic image was being projected—church bells announcing the resurrection of Christ.

Example 1.3B:
*Windhaager Mass—Credo—*bars 1–5

Cre–do in   u– num   De–   um

The *Sanctus* is very short, only twenty bars, and presents the most extensive and melodically important horn parts to this point in the work. Particularly in the first few phrases, they double the melodic line and are coupled with it using a mixture of sixths and fifths. In the manuscript the voice part for this movement is marked *"doppelt Gesang,"* indicating that at least two singers are required for performance (Schulze 1986, 3). Wagner sees this as another expressive device, illustrating Bruckner's knowledge of the liturgy (Wagner 1996, 23). The *Sanctus* is associated with the celebration of the Eucharist. Bruckner's doubling of the vocal line apparently was a metaphor for including everyone in that celebration.

The *Benedictus*, in E-flat major, is the only movement in a key other than the tonic. Lyrically constructed, it employs a lovely original melody and text setting that is much less syllabic than the rest of the work.[6] At the words *"in nomine Domini,"* Bruckner employs a dominant pedal—another foreshadowing of his mature technique (Göllerich/Auer 1974, I: 190).

Bruckner returned to the hymn-like texture of earlier movements at the *Agnus Dei*. The three-fold repetition of the title words, set in sequential two-bar phrases near the end of the movement, adds a fine sense of pathos to these bars, and the final notes of the movement recall the closing of the *Credo*—a small but effective touch of long-range musical integration.

The frequent appearances of unison passages throughout this work are an additional hallmark of Bruckner's later style. In his mature compositions such passages are usually climactic in nature. In this early work unison writing sometimes identifies important textual phrases (such as the "bell motive" at the words *"Cum Sancto Spiritu"* in the *Gloria*, and at the *"Et resurrexit ..."* in the *Credo*), and at other times its appearance seems rather arbitrary.

In the context of this study, the use of the horns requires some comment. Wagner suggests that Bruckner included them in this work to contrast with strings, and to identify it with "what is normal, close to life" (Wagner 1996, 23). In other words, the horns associated this mass with the common people who made up the congregation for which it was intended and who were, of course, Bruckner's own stock. Unquestionably, their presence adds a warm, familiar timbre to the music, and helps to clarify the harmony. As previously observed, they function melodically

---

[6]As with previous movements, the text of the *Benedictus* is truncated. The *Hosanna*, which normally concludes this movement and is required liturgically, is missing from Bruckner's setting (Schulze 1986, 3). This omission is curious, since Bruckner was very familiar with the Catholic liturgy.

only in the *Sanctus*, where, for several phrases, they double the alto's melodic line in parallel fifths and sixths.

The *Mass in C Major* has received considerable attention in Bruckner research. The modest means employed in its creation belie a clearly formed aesthetic concept and substantial musical imagination. Although written in difficult circumstances, it "expresses in a touching way all the happiness of humble escape into the inner self, which can be found in a person who does not worship God in a dogmatic way but rather recognizes Him in his own experience" (Göllerich/Auer 1974, I: 170). Flashes of individuality reveal a musical aspiration reaching well beyond the composer's technique and training at this point. Analysis shows that the attention lavished on this modest work is justified, not merely because it was Bruckner's first extended composition, but also because of its interesting and prophetic musical ideas.

Chapter 2

St. Florian 1845–55

In May 1845 Bruckner completed the final exam for assistant teachers and was therefore prepared for a position at a larger and more prestigious school. An appropriate placement appeared almost immediately at St. Florian, and Bruckner returned to his former home the following September. In addition to teaching duties, he served as deputy organist to Anton Kattinger, who had been his teacher in the 1830s (Watson 1977, 9).

Bruckner's second stay at St. Florian lasted for ten years, and was of immense importance to his future. During this time he gradually abandoned the classroom and committed himself to music. This career path was initiated by the appointment itself, which included specific musical responsibilities for the first time. However, it received its first major advancement a few years later. In 1848 Kattinger was transferred to Kremsmünster, and Bruckner was promoted to "provisional organist"[1] at St. Florian (Schönzeler 1970, 31). Although music was assuming an ever-growing place in his life, Bruckner embraced it rather cautiously. Throughout the 1840s and early 1850s, he continued to add teaching qualifications to his personal portfolio, including: a testimonial for Latin studies in 1852, a major certificate for organ playing in October 1854, and completion of the requirements for high school teachers in January 1855 (Watson 1977, 141). However, by 1855 many of his friends were advising him to leave the seclusion of St. Florian, and to find a position

---

[1]Researchers are divided on whether Bruckner was ever given the full position. Cooke and Nowak claim that he was promoted to "official organist" in 1851 (Cooke/Nowak 1985, 4–5). However, Doernberg refers to Bruckner's last salary receipt from St. Florian, dated December 22, 1855, in which he still signed himself as "provisional organist" (Doernberg 1960, 34). Doernberg's contention is supported by Bruckner himself. The title page to his *Missa solemnis*, written in 1854, is signed "Anton Bruckner, provisional organist" (Göllerich/Auer 1974, II/1: 155). Regardless of the truth in this matter, it remains clear that his replacement of Kattinger in 1848 was a major step in directing him toward a musical career.

where his musical talent could be nurtured. Ultimately, it took direct intervention by one of these friends, August Dürrnberger, to propel him into such a post when it became available (Schönzeler 1970, 35).

Musically, the St. Florian years illustrate a marked evolution in Bruckner's compositional activity and ability. Since his musical responsibilities gradually increased during his tenure, most of the more than forty titles dating from this period were written during the early 1850s. While the earlier works (interesting though many of them are) are largely the products of an apprentice learning his craft, the later works show substantial growth in sophistication and self-assurance. His promotion to "provisional organist" in 1848 was an important watershed. Bruckner apparently saw this promotion as recognition of his musicianship, and it appears to have given him substantial confidence in his compositional abilities. Within a few months he had begun his *Requiem* in D minor—his first truly large-scale composition and probably his first significant work.

For wind researchers and conductors, the St. Florian years are of considerable interest. During this time Bruckner produced no fewer than eight wind works, all of which are interesting, and several of which are significant contributions to the repertoire.

MISSA EX G-MOLL PRO QUADRAGESIMA—WAB 140

This work, which is believed to date from late 1845, is only a sketch of the opening bars of the *Kyrie*. However, despite their fragmentary state, these seventeen bars demonstrate how far the composer's skills had developed in just a few years. While the *Windhaager Mass* was conceived in a resolutely homophonic style, the few extant bars of the G minor mass show that the composer's abilities now permitted him to think contrapuntally. The manuscript includes only an organ part, *arpeggiating* the underlying harmony, and the melody, which is divided between altos and sopranos. This sharing of the melody implies that additional contrapuntal lines were planned.

Also of interest from the point of view of this study, is the scoring—chorus, organ, and trombones. The choice of instruments may well have been determined by the day for which the work was intended—the first Sunday of Lent (Göllerich/-Auer 1974, II/1: 63). Bruckner may have wanted the sombre sound of the trombones to mark this serious occasion. However, it must also be noted that this scoring became a particular favourite of the composer. Much of the liturgical music from all parts of his life employs precisely this instrumentation, or a near derivative of it.

ZWEI AEQUALE—WAB 114, 149

In January 1847 Bruckner's mother informed him of the passing away of his godmother, Rosalie Mayrhofer. Ms. Mayrhofer's death apparently stimulated the composition of the two *Aequale* for trombone trio.[2] In fact, only the piece now identified as *Aequali No. 1* (WAB 114) can be precisely dated, but, since both works exhibit identical style, it seems reasonable to assume that they were written at the same time. The manuscripts consist of parts only without scores. The bass trombone part for *Aequali No. 2* (WAB 149) is lost and has been reconstructed by the musicologist Hans Bauernfeind (Proffitt 1991, 2). These two short and solemn works are very popular with trombonists, are frequently performed, and have been recorded several times.

Although intended as funeral music, Göllerich and Auer feel that Bruckner's *Aequale* express hope and comfort rather than grief (Göllerich/Auer 1974, II/1: 63). This contention is supported by the composer's harmonic choices. While both pieces are in C minor, large sections of them are in major mode and virtually all phrases cadence on major chords, bringing a serene, reverent quality to both works. This devout character is enhanced by musical style. Like chorales, all cadences are clearly marked with long notes and *fermatas*, and uneven phrase lengths suggest chant, although no specific liturgical melodies are utilized. Dynamics are very effectively employed. In *Aequali No. 2*, a phrase in major mode is echoed in the tonic minor at a quieter dynamic.

Example 2.1:
Aequali No. 2—bars 17–20

As observed in other works by Bruckner from this time period, the harmony is tonally functional, but emphasizes sudden shifts to third-related key areas. In *Aequali No 1* the relative major and tonic major are prominently featured. These areas also appear in *Aequali No. 2*, but the major sub-mediant (A-flat major) also assumes an important role.

Beyond these substantial similarities, the two pieces show distinctive characteristics. The melody in *Aequali No. 1* is virtually always doubled in parallel sixths or thirds between alto and tenor trombone. This degree of emphasis on melody draws the listener to the linear quality of this music. In *Aequali No. 2* the melody is largely in tenor trombone while alto and bass have primarily a harmonic function. "Hiding" the melody in this way emphasizes the chordal character of this piece. Also, in this second work phrase lengths are even more varied than in its companion piece. In fact, no regular phrase length is established at all.

---

[2]According to Bruckner's birth certificate, Ms. Mayrhofer was present at his birth (Göllerich/Auer 1974, I:54).

Apparently, Bruckner's *Aequale* and other similar music was performed at the outer gate to St. Florian, where the dead were placed until a priest could undertake the consecration (Göllerich/Auer 1974, II/1: 63). Bruckner's choice of instruments and musical style seem singularly appropriate to such a function. The sound of the trombones would be suitably solemn and resonant within the enclosed space surrounding the gate, and the simple homophonic textures, using primarily long notes and recalling the music of worship, would be unobtrusive but consoling to grieving relatives.

PSALM 114 (116)—WAB 36

Psalm 114 (116) is Bruckner's first indisputable masterpiece for chorus and winds. Composed in 1852 and scored for an unusual five-voice choir with two alto parts accompanied by three trombones, it is among the least known and least frequently performed of his works. The extant primary sources are quite extensive. The autograph score, one copy of each part and an incomplete fair copy of the score are preserved at St. Florian, and additional scores and parts, dating from early in this century, can be found in several Viennese libraries (Hawkshaw 1997, i–ii). A facsimile reproduction of the autograph is published in Göllerich and Auer.[3] However, a complete fair copy of the score was also prepared and remains in the possession of the descendants of the dedicatee, the Viennese *Kapellmeister* Ignaz Assmayer (Göllerich/Auer 1974, II/1: 136).

Bruckner met Assmayer in 1851 in Vienna (Watson 1977, 11). The *Kapellmeister*, who had a reputation for aloofness, apparently received Bruckner with warmth and friendliness, which was greatly appreciated by the rather insecure young man. Some months later, on July 30, 1852, Bruckner wrote to Assmayer:

Above all, my congratulations on the occasion of your honourable name-day celebration.... Your friendly reception will remain forever unforgettable to me.... As a small proof of the fulfilment of your beneficial instruction, I have taken the liberty of dedicating the enclosed psalm, as a weak attempt, to the very Honourable on the occasion of his name-day; I would like to ask [you] not to be offended by my weakness and to show mercy and indulgence in every way. (Göllerich/Auer 1974, II/1: 137–38)

In a postscript to the same letter, Bruckner indicated that the new work had had a reading in St. Florian: "I had [some] musicians try out the psalm in the music room of the abbey, even musicians from Vienna who were experts participated, and it was received with a lot of approval" (Göllerich/Auer 1974, II/1: 137–38).

The set of parts in the St. Florian archive display performers markings, and undoubtedly were prepared for this "reading." These parts represent an intermediate stage in the creation of this work—between the autograph and the fair copy presented to Assmayer (Hawkshaw 1997, ii). In the autograph, the voice and the trombone parts occasionally divide. During the reading, which seems to be the only

---

[3]Göllerich/Auer 1974, II/2: 151–77.

time that the work was heard in the composer's lifetime, Bruckner apparently decided which of these alternatives was best, since the presentation copy contains no divided parts. The only documented performance of *Psalm 114 (116)* was conducted by August Göllerich in Linz on April 1, 1906 (Göllerich/Auer 1974, II/1: 366–67).[4]

The confusion about the numbering of this psalm originates in the conflict of psalm numeration between the Vulgate and most Protestant Bibles. The text is the first nine verses of what is considered to be *Psalm 116* in the Revised Standard (Protestant) Version of the Bible and in Hebrew texts. This numbering system has achieved broad acceptance among liturgical writers. However, the Vulgate numeration, which would have been most familiar to Bruckner, draws on the original Greek translations of these texts. *Psalm 116* is divided in two. The first nine verses, precisely those set by Bruckner, are considered *Psalm 114*, while the additional verses make up *Psalm 115* (Werner et al. 1980, 320). This text division is confirmed in the *Liber Usualis*. Although Bruckner apparently was aware of the conflict in numeration, he was a practicing Roman Catholic, and considered this work to be *Psalm 114*.[5]

The structure of this psalm setting, which is quite simple in concept, is

---

[4]The English conductor Matthew Best performed and recorded *Psalm 114 (116)* with the Corydon Singers and the English Chamber Orchestra in 1987 (Hyperion CD—CDA66245). For his purposes Maestro Best edited the difficult-to-read, and in some aspects incomplete, manuscript. Maestro Best's performances in England were undoubtedly the first outside Austria, and may well have been the first since 1906.

A reference score, edited by Paul Hawkshaw, appeared in 1997 as Band 20, No. 1, of the Collected Works. For his edition, Hawkshaw drew primarily on the dedication score sent by Bruckner to Assmayer, since this score best represents the composer's final thoughts on the work (Hawkshaw 1997, i–ii).

[5]The title of Bruckner's manuscript, at least as it appears in facsimile in Göllerich/Auer, displays both numbers; however, 116 is in smaller writing and is in brackets. The verses set by Bruckner are:

Alleluia!

I love the Lord, because He hath heard my voice and my supplications.   [1]

Because He hath inclined His ear unto me, therefore will I call upon Him as long as I live.   [2]

The sorrows of death compassed me, and the pains of hell gat hold upon me: I found trouble and sorrow.   [3]

Then called I upon the name of the Lord; O Lord, I beseech thee, deliver my soul. [4]

Gracious is the Lord, and righteous; yea, our Lord is merciful.   [5]

The Lord preserveth the simple: I was brought low, and he helped me.   [6]

Return unto thy rest, O my soul; for the Lord hath dealt bountifully with thee.   [7]

For Thou hast delivered my soul from death, mine eyes from tears, and my feet from falling.   [8]

I will walk before the Lord in the land of the living.   [9]

(Simpson 1987, 6)

grounded in liturgical practice. It opens with an *Alleluia* in four phrases that functions like an *Antiphon*, and individual verses of the psalm (with the exception of verses seven and eight) are clearly separated by strong cadences and/or a few beats of silence. They display substantial contrasts of timbre, texture, and harmony. According to the *Liber Usualis*, *Psalm 114* has two functions within the liturgy, both associated with Vespers. As a Ferial[6] psalm it is read at Vespers on Mondays, and it also forms part of the Vespers ceremony of the Office for the Dead (*Liber Usualis* 1952, 280, 1772). Bruckner's setting does not seem to have been intended for either of these ceremonies. However, when *Psalm 114* is read at Monday Vespers during Paschal time,[7] its *Antiphon* is a four-phrase *Alleluia*. Paschal time would have concluded shortly before Bruckner began composing this work.[8] This ritual may have been foremost in his memory and provided the stimulus for his *Alleluia* as a preface to the setting itself. The *Liber Usualis* may also furnish a clue as to the dearth of specific liturgical melodies in this work, even though a number of melodic fragments are reminiscent of plainchant. The five psalms designated for use at Monday Vespers are *read* not sung. Chants are provided for the *Antiphons* but not for the psalms themselves.

Bruckner himself provides evidence that this setting grew out of personal inspiration. In 1852 he had become deeply discouraged by the lack of recognition accorded music, and consequently himself, at St. Florian. In his letter quoted above, he complained to Assmayer:

I don't have anyone here to whom I could open my heart, I am being misunderstood in various ways as well, which is secretly a hardship for me. Our monastery treats music, and consequently musicians as well, with absolute indifference ... I can never be happy here and am not allowed to show any of my plans. (Göllerich/Auer 1974, II/1: 137–38).

Immersed in a distressed state of mind, Bruckner seems to have turned to the reassuring words of this psalm for encouragement and consolation.

Bruckner's four-phrase *Alleluia*, which serves as an *Antiphon* to the psalm setting, is homophonically constructed. To ensure that his hymn-like melody would be easily heard, the composer wrote it into the alto trombone doubled by a different selection of voices for virtually every phrase. For the first two phrases, sopranos and first altos are assigned the melody. At the third phrase the first altos take it over, and during the final phrase it is transferred to second altos. For three of its four phrases, the music is essentially devoid of accidentals (other than the single sharp in the key signature and a D-sharp that ornaments the third of the chord at the cadence of the

---

[6]Associated with the days of the week, not Sundays.

[7]Easter Sunday to Whitsun inclusive (*Liber Usualis* 1952, 12). Whitsun, or Whitsunday, is the seventh Sunday after Easter.

[8]In 1852 Easter was celebrated on April 11. Paschal Time would have concluded on Sunday, May 30.

second phrase), allowing it to conform harmonically to e-*aeolian*.[9] Its modal character is especially conspicuous in the minor dominant sonorities, which confer a rather archaic sound on this entire passage. At the fourth phrase D-sharp and G-sharp are added, permitting the music to cadence in E major. The cadences of all four phrases, D major, B major, D major, and E major, respectively, emphasize the dominant, mediant, and sub-mediant of the eventual tonic, G major.

Verses one and two ("I love the Lord ..." and "Because He hath inclined His ear ...") employ variations of the same musical material. *A cappella* scoring, a polyphonic texture, quiet dynamics, and simple diatonic harmony give these verses a gentle, devout character that is a fine reflection of the text. Derivatives of this material reappear at verse five ("Gracious is the Lord ..."), and at the second half of verse seven ("for the Lord hath dealt bountifully with thee"). Since all of these stanzas describe a kind and merciful God, Bruckner's repetition of his initial idea is appropriate to the words. It also provides a very satisfying sense of musical unity.

The first half of verse three ("The sorrows of death ...") is very dramatic. The trombones enter at *fortissimo*, the vocal parts are initially compressed to a single unison line comprised of very wide skips, and the harmony switches suddenly from D major to D minor, then progresses quickly through a series of third related keys.

Example 2.2:
Psalm 114—bars 40–49

Abrupt shifts between major and minor chords with the same root have been

---

[9]Modal writing is not unusual in Bruckner's oeuvre. The first of the two *Asperges me* of 1845 is in *aeolian* mode; the hymn *Jam lucis* and the *Pange lingua* of 1868 are both *phrygian*; the Gradual *Os justi* from 1879 is *lydian*; and several extended sections of modal harmony appear in the *E-minor Mass* (Watson 1977, 92, 98–99).

encountered before in the works under review, but in all previous cases major chords at loud dynamics were answered by quietly articulated minor chords. Bruckner's reversing of this procedure is striking and was inspired by the words, which present the anguished cry of a soul in distress, pleading for divine intervention. The loud dynamics, angular melody, and primarily minor harmonies depict this sentiment in a particularly graphic way. The second half of this stanza ("I found trouble and sorrow") begins as a double canon in coupled thirds that contrasts female and male voices. Although initially unaccompanied, it ultimately involves the entire ensemble in a profoundly moving passage that prominently features minor seventh chords, and immeasurably heightens the sense of suffering expressed by these words. The music of both parts of this verse clearly had personal significance for Bruckner, reflecting in a deeply expressive way the "trouble and sorrow" he was enduring at the time of its composition. However, aside from the music's individual reference, the several contrasts of texture and the memorable timbral changes appearing in this verse provide a gratifying variety of sonority that demonstrates Bruckner's fine musical judgment.

The fourth verse brings additional textural variety. The first phrase of the text ("Then I called upon the name of the Lord") is set in a series of parallel sixth chords, like *fauxbourdon*, and employs only the three female voices. The music sounds like a hymn, and, considering that the words are a prayer, seems highly appropriate. The second textual phrase ("O Lord; O Lord, I beseech thee ...") utilizes the rest of the ensemble—the male voices and the trombones. Loud dynamics and closed position harmonies give this segment a dramatic character that recalls the beginning of verse three and reflects Bruckner's confidence that God will hear him and respond. Verse five, where the music of the initial verses is recalled, would seem to affirm that that confidence was justified—that God had indeed responded.

Verse six ("The Lord preserves the simple ...") begins like verse four—in simple block chord harmonies using only the female voices. The second phrase ("I was brought low ...") is substantially extended through a long E major cadence, during which the words "and He helped me" are repeated several times, presumably another affirmation of the composer's unshakable Faith.

Bruckner evidently felt that verses seven and eight comprised a single entity, since he bound these verses together in his setting. Verse seven commences with a homophonic declamation of the text ("Return unto thy rest ...") using a single chord (C major), and supported by the trombones. The music of its second phrase, another assertion of the benevolence of God, again recalls verse one, and leads directly into verse eight ("For Thou has delivered my soul ..."), which, not surprisingly considering the text, is the climax of this part of the work. Göllerich and Auer describe this passage as "radiant" (Göllerich/Auer 1974, II/1: 141), and its widely spaced chords forming consecutive cadences in the surprising keys of E-flat major and F minor are indeed glorious. The rest of verse eight is much more subdued, which reinforces the climactic nature of the preceding measures, and perhaps reflects the fact that the previous despair is now merely a memory.

Example 2.3:
Psalm 114—bars 106–9

The final words ("and my feet from falling") are set as a two-voice canon over a dominant pedal. These measures provide an effective bridge to the final verse, which consists of a large-scale *fugue* in the tonic (G major). The imitative texture and the tonal stability provided by the pedal allow the transition to be smoothly accomplished.

The final verse ("I will walk before the Lord ...") is a five-voice double *fugue* that extends to more than eighty bars—nearly equivalent in length to the preceding eight verses. The two subjects are immediately presented against each other in counterpoint and clearly display their derivation from the music of J. S. Bach.

Example 2.4:
Psalm 114—bars 119–23

Considering the words, and having already noted Bruckner's penchant for poetic realization of text, it is tempting to see these two themes as representing God (the stately initial subject) and the composer himself (the second "busy" subject). Similarly, one might consider Bruckner's decision to set these final words in *fugue* as a means of expanding the reference of his composition from the personal to the universal. While this section starts with only the composer and his God, other voices soon appear and continue to appear throughout the numerous episodes making up this broad musical structure. The deeply personal nature of much of this work has already been noted. Perhaps Bruckner's *fugue*, with its many voices, was intended to counterbalance the personal reference and to broaden the work's scope to include all humanity walking joyfully with God "in the land of the living."

From a strictly musical point of view, the *fugue* is mostly successful. While a few transitions sound awkward (for example, bars 179–80), most of the episodes and middle entries flow smoothly one to the next. The culmination is a substantial *stretto* (bars 180–95) that includes the first subject in both its primary form and in inversion, as well as fragments of subject two, also in inversion. Following the *stretto*, the work ends abruptly.[10] The counterpoint is simplified to homophony, then, already a Bruckner fingerprint, to unison. The plagal cadence that closes the work is less than convincing.

Bruckner's *Psalm 114* is an aurally pleasing and expressive composition that does not deserve the near oblivion to which it has been relegated. Certainly, some of the music is derivative. Göllerich and Auer relate the end of verse one to Mozart, and the beginning of verse seven to Wagner, even though Bruckner could not have heard any of Wagner's music in 1852 (Göllerich/Auer 1974, II/1: 139, 141). The influence of J. S. Bach pervades the *fugue* that completes the composition. However, much of this work is truly inspired. It projects a profound understanding of the text, captivates the ear with interesting harmonies and varied timbres and textures, and demonstrates that Bruckner, even at this early point in his compositional career, was capable of creating appealing and compelling music. *Psalm 114* represents another important step in his slow progress toward a purely musical career.

CANTATA: HEIL, VATER! DIR ZUM HOHEN FESTE—WAB 61

Bruckner composed this seven-movement[11] *cantata* for the nameday, September 29, 1852, of his friend Michael Arneth, the Prelate of St. Florian.[12] The manuscript bears the completion date September 27, 1852, which allowed only two days for the parts to be copied and the work rehearsed. The scoring for male quartet, mixed choir, two trumpets, three horns, and bass trombone is interesting and may provide a clue to the nature of the first performance. The single trombone functions mostly as the bass voice of a horn quartet.[13] Trombones have a long

---

[10]The abrupt ending is a stylistic fingerprint in all of Bruckner's music. Robert Simpson believes this idea originated in the composer's many years in the service of religious music, and was intended to exploit the resonant acoustics of large churches (Simpson 1946, 34).

[11]Movements two and three are repeated as movements four and five. The text is different in movements two and four, even though the music is identical. Movement five is an exact repetition of movement three.

[12]Bruckner had written a cantata to commemorate Arneth's nameday in 1851. This work, entitled *Entsagen* (WAB 14), was scored for mixed choir, soloists and organ (Göllerich/Auer 1974, II/1: 43–44).

[13]This particular scoring, three horns and bass trombone, occurs frequently in scores dating from the first half of the nineteenth century. The register in which these trombone parts are written lies low in the horn's harmonic series, where the individual harmonics are widely spaced. Many of the notes would have been available on early nineteenth century valveless horns only by hand stopping, and others would not have been playable at all. For bass trombone, however, these notes appear in one of its best and most complete registers,

(continued...)

association with liturgical music, a correlation that Bruckner was to utilize in his religious compositions throughout his life. The lack of pure trombone sound here may suggest that Bruckner considered this work to be secular not sacred, and that it was intended for performance at an outdoor ceremony rather than in the church. On the other hand, the music is largely celebratory in nature. Perhaps the composer felt that the trombone sonority was too solemn for this particular occasion.

No fewer than three different texts have been applied to this music, and considerable confusion about their ordering has been absorbed into the Bruckner literature over the years. Paul Hawkshaw has investigated this issue in detail and has provided convincing evidence for the following chronology. The text, *Heil, Vater! Dir zum hohen Feste*, was the original, intended for the 1852 performance. This text is quoted in its entirety below. In 1857 Bruckner revised the work for performance at the nameday celebration of Friedrich Mayr, Arneth's successor as Prelate of St. Florian. He adapted the music to a new text, *Auf Brüder! auf zur frohen Feier!*, and made a few other changes as well. This text and the revisions it precipitated will be discussed in the next chapter. A third text, *Heil dir zum schönen Erstlingsfeste*, was applied to the original 1852 score and was performed during a *Primiz*, the first Mass celebrated by a newly ordained priest, in Kremsmünster in 1870. Bruckner apparently had no hand in this revision and therefore it will not be discussed in this study (Hawkshaw 1984, 214–20).

The original text was written by the canon at St. Florian, Ernst Marinelli:

Heil Vater! Dir zum hohen Feste,
Es reichen wir und werte Gäste
Des Dankes und der Liebe Preis
Dir durch die Gunst der Musen

Hail father! To you on this noble celebration,
We and worthy guests donate to you
The prize for gratitude and Love
Through the favour of the Muses.

Dir schlägt so treu und wahr und heiß
Das Herz in jedum Busen.

To you the heart beats faithful, true and fervently in every bosom.

An dreißig Jahre mögens sein,
Da standest du als Vater ein
Für uns in Gott zu sorgen
Und alle, die sich dir vertrauf,
Die freudig auf dein Wort gebaut,
Sie waren wohl geborgen.

It should be about thirty years,
Since you vouched as father
To care for us in God
And all who believed in you,
And happily trusted your word,
They were well sheltered.

Drum bringen wir mit Jubel heut',
Was jedes Herz an Liebe beut,
Was jeder Mund für dich erfleht
Und jeder Blick dir froh gesteht
Am Weihaltar des Dankes dar.

Therefore we bring as an offering today with joy,
What every heart offers in Love,
What every mouth evokes for you,
And every eye confesses to you with joy,

---

[13](...continued)
making it an excellent bass voice for the horn quartet.

On the blessed alter of thanks.

Du wirktest treu und bieder hier,	You acted faithfully and honestly here,
Drum sahst du in der Canonie	Therefore you saw within the Canonics
Manch edle Brust erscheinen,	Many a noble heart appear,
Du hast gelöst die schwere Pflicht	You bore the heavy burden
Und darum auch vergessen's nicht	And that is why your people will not
Die Deinen!	forget it!
Sie bringen dir mit Jubel heut'	Today they bring to you with jubilation,
Was jedes Herz an Liebe beut,	What every heart offers in Love,
Was jeder Mund für dich erfleht,	What every mouth evokes for you,
Und jeder Blick dir froh gesteht,	And every eye confesses to you with joy,
Sie rufen heut' im Brüderchor	Today as a brotherly choir they shout
Für dich den Dank des Herrn empor.	For you, the gratitude of the Lord.

(Collected Works, 22/I/No. 3a: 57–75,   (Translation by Ruth Thomas)
and Hawkshaw 1984, 216).

Musically, this *cantata* represents something of a backward step for Bruckner. Most of the harmony is conventionally diatonic, and this work displays little of the skilfully constructed, expressive counterpoint or the timbral/textural imagination evident in *Psalm 114*. Much of the melodic development involves simple repetition or sequence. All of the above suggest that this piece was written quickly with little time for creative preparation or revision.

The work consists of two movement types. Choruses using the entire ensemble alternate with *a capella* movements for the male quartet. For the most part, the choruses adhere closely to the tonic (D major) with occasional secondary dominant harmonies. The quartets are mostly in the subdominant (G major), and are somewhat more chromatic. The final quartet, movement six, begins in the surprising key of B-flat major and is less conventionally diatonic than earlier movements. Similarly, the final chorus briefly moves further afield harmonically by cadencing successively in B-flat major and C major before returning to the tonic (D major).

Simple though it is, this work does display some marks of Bruckner's style. Two horn passages recur frequently, providing, as would similar passages in later works, considerable musical unity.

Example 2.5A:
Cantata: Heil, Vater! ... Feste—bars 1–2

Example 2.5B:
Cantata: Heil, Vater! ... Feste—bars 14–15

All movements after the first make extensive use of a distinctive melodic motive.

Example 2.6:
Cantata: Heil, Vater! ... Feste—bars 25–27

Unison passges and downward skips in dotted rhythms appear, sometimes surprisingly, in all the choruses.

Göllerich and Auer have noted another interesting detail about this composition.[14] The horn motive quoted in Example 2.5B, which sounds like Mendelssohn, recurs just before the *Qui tollis* in the *Gloria* of the *E-minor Mass* of 1866.

Example 2.7:
E-minor Mass—Gloria—bars 63–65

In both cases these passages are continued by the female voices of the choir, either exactly as stated by the horns or in an obvious variation.

With its rudimentary harmonic sequences, simple textures, and melodic development based on repetition and sequence, this is an undistinguished work. Bruckner, however, was deeply indebted to Michael Arneth and obviously wanted to

---

[14]Göllerich and Auer also draw a parallel between the chordal structure at the words "*Da standest du als Vater ein*" in the first quartet, and the beginning of the Pilgrim's Chorus in Act III of Wagner's *Tannhäuser*—at the words "*O Heimat, ich schauen*" (Göllerich/Auer 1974, II/1: 129). Since neither of these composers could possibly have heard any of the other's music at this time, and the concurrence between the passages is far from exact, it seems pointless to draw this comparison.

play a major role in the celebration of his nameday. He produced a utilitarian, celebratory composition that had surprising endurance, surviving as it did through three revisions. Today, it maintains a degree of historical significance, but is of limited musical interest.

LIBERA ME—WAB 22

On March 24, 1854, the St. Florian community was saddened by the death of its Prelate, Michael Arneth. Bruckner felt the loss especially deeply since Arneth had been a consistent supporter, often intervening on his behalf when difficulties arose in his personal or professional life. For the funeral, Bruckner composed two short choral works, the *Libera me* in F minor, and the gravesong, *Vor Arneths Grab*. These two compositions share some material, and both contain elements that would become hallmarks of the composer's mature style.

The manuscript of the *Libera me* bears the completion date, March 24, 1854. Since it could not have been written in a single day, this date suggests that Arneth's death was expected, at least by Bruckner. It received its first performance on March 28 during the ceremony of Absolution that followed the Requiem Mass. Scored for mixed chorus, three trombones, cello, double bass,[15] and organ, it is at once conventional and inventive.

The form of this work was determined by the Latin text.[16] At the smallest

---

[15]Bruckner's inclusion of the two stringed instruments is interesting. They double the bass line throughout, but since this line is also written into the organ and, at times, the bass trombone, they can rarely be heard. They do add considerable resonance to the sound of the ensemble, and the addition of string instruments to the bass lines of wind ensemble music was a common practice throughout the eighteenth and nineteenth centuries. Bruckner apparently was aware of this tradition.

[16]The text is:

Libera me, Domine, de morte aeterna, in die illa tremenda:
Quando coeli movendi sunt et terra:
Dum veneris judicare saeculum per ignem.

Tremens factus sum ergo et timeo, dum discussivo venerit, atque ventura ira.
Quando coeli movendi sunt et terra.

Dies illa, dies irae, calamitatis et miseriae, dies magna et amara valde.
Dum veneris judicare saeculum per ignem.

Requiem aeternam dona eis, Domine: et lux perpetua luceat eis.

Libera, Domine, etc ...

(continued...)

structural level each textual phrase is separated by cadences and a few beats of silence, while at larger levels verses are identified by dramatic changes of texture. Bruckner chose a simple hymn-like style for the first and fourth verses. The second verse begins as a five-voice *fugato*. A countersubject in parallel sixths is applied against every entry, and chromatic inflections in all of the melodic material create a rapid harmonic rhythm of largely step-wise progressions. Both the melodic content and the harmony are reminiscent of Mendelssohn. The third verse displays a variety of imitative textures, including antiphony between female and male voices, and responsive textures similar to those encountered in music of the high Renaissance.

All of these are the compositional procedures historically associated with church music, and Bruckner largely avoided the temptation of indulging in tone painting—except perhaps for setting the words "*illa tremenda*" (dreadful day) at *fortissimo*, and half-step clashes at *Dies illa, dies irae* (day of anger)—even though the text provides numerous opportunities. Perhaps he felt that the sanctity of the occasion precluded such an approach, and turned instead to traditional means and earlier models, notably Mozart. For example, at the *illa tremenda: Quando coeli*, the chord sequence is virtually identical with that of the *Gere curam* in the *Confutatis* of Mozart's *Requiem* (Göllerich/Auer 1974, II/1: 154).

Example 2.8A:
Libera me—bars 8–10

---

[16](...continued)
[Deliver me, O Lord, from everlasting death, on that dreadful day,
When the heavens and the earth shall be moved:
When Thou shall come to judge the world by fire.

I quake with fear and I tremble, awaiting the day of account and the wrath to come.
When the heavens and the earth shall be moved.

That day, the day of anger, of calamity, of misery, that great day and most bitter.
When Thou shall come to judge the world by fire.

Eternal rest grant them, O Lord: and let perpetual light shine upon them.

Deliver me, O Lord, etc ...]

Example 2.8B:
Mozart—*Requiem*—*Confutatis*—bars 34–35

However, even though the conception of the work is conventional, the harmonic materials are often far from orthodox. Important cadences occur on both the mediant (A-flat major) and on the sub-mediant (D-flat major). The words "*Quando coeli movendi sunt et terra*" are set to a bold sequence of third related chords.

Example 2.9:
***Libera me*—bars 9–12**

During the *fugato* at verse two, Bruckner introduces the augmented sixth chord as a substitute for the dominant seventh, a harmonic strategy that was to become a particular favourite in later years (Simpson 1967, 125), appearing with great regularity in, for example, the symphonies.

Example 2.10:
***Libera me*—bars 20, 22**

In the imitative counterpoint that makes up verse three (*Dies illa, dies irae*), several entries into the texture are a half step above an already sounding part. These clashes add tremendous poignacy to the music, are aurally surprising, and will be encountered again in later works, notably the *E-minor Mass*. Also surprising are the contrapuntally generated polychords that appear momentarily from time to time at various points during the piece.

Example 2.11:
Libera me—bars 42–47

Apart from its significance as a precursor to Bruckner's mature style, the F minor *Libera me* is effective on its own terms. The music is heartfelt and profound, and is a gracious, if rather austere, rendering of the text.

VOR ARNETHS GRAB—WAB 53

This work, like the *Libera me* in F minor, was written for the funeral of Prelate Michael Arneth in St. Florian on March 28, 1854. It was scored for male chorus and three trombones, and uses a text written for the occasion by canon Ernst Marinelli:

Brüder, trocknet Eure Zähren,
Stillt der Schmerzen herbes Leid,
Liebe kann sich auch bewähren
Durch Ergebungs-Innigkeit.

Brothers, dry your tears,
Soothe the bitter pain and suffering,
Love can prove itself as well
Through sincere surrendering.

Wohl ist dies das letzte Schauen
Auf die Leiche und den Sarg
Doch die Seele, die sie barg,
Triumphiert durch Gottvertrauen.

Indeed, this is the last glance
At the corpse and the coffin
However, the soul which it housed
Has triumphed through its trust in God.

Lasset uns den Herren preisen,
Der den Edelsten erwählt
Und für uns, die armen Waisen
Auch den Himmel offen hält.

Let us praise the Lord,
Who chooses the most noble
And leaves open for us poor orphans
Heaven as well.

Wollen hier am Grab geloben
Treue, Recht und frommen Sinn,
Daß der Selige dort oben,
Hat sich unser Geist erhoben,
Uns zum Vater führe hin.

Let us vow here at the gravesite
Faith, Justice and pious mind,
So that the blessed one up there in Heaven,
Will lead us to the Father,
When our spirit is risen.

(Göllerich/Auer 1974, II/1: 152)

(Translation by Ruth Thomas)

As is clear from the title and the text, this is a gravesong. However, it displays little of the mournful character one might expect. Like the words, the music largely avoids the expression of grief, focusing instead on confidence in the Christian teachings about resurrection and salvation. The harmony is largely diatonic, with a predominance of major sonorities. The voicing is very resonant, with a wide space maintained between the two lowest voices most of the time. Overall, the piece has an elevated, reassuring quality that was apparently intended to draw the mourners out of their sorrow and encourage them to rely on their Christian Faith.

Despite its functional origin, this brief work, too, contains portents of Bruckner's mature style. It begins with a melodic fragment that provides the material for the entire piece.

Example 2.12:
Vor Arneths Grab—bars 1–3

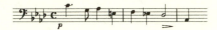

As in many later compositions by this composer, this root motive appears in the bass voices (doubled by second trombone), under a pedal. More important, however, is its ambiguous tonality—both A-flat major and F minor are implied. A-flat major is eventually confirmed as the tonic, but not until the end of the first verse (bar 8). Göllerich and Auer make much of the fact that the work ends in F major, the major sub-mediant key (Göllerich/Auer 1974, II/1: 153), and it is clear now that these scholars had noticed a very important principle at work in this brief composition. Since the work will end in F major, the suggestion of both keys in these initial bars is clearly an example of the "double-tonic" or "tonal pairing" procedures that are now recognized as a central element in late nineteenth-century tonal practice.[17] However, within the context of a number of cadences in third-related keys the ambiguous tonality does not sound especially unusual, even though it is unique among Bruckner's early compositions.

---

[17]Robert Bailey is credited with evolving this concept for his analyses of the music of Wagner. Bailey noticed that Wagner preferred to foreshadow the overall tonal movement within an entire act of his operas at the very beginning of the overture. Thus, the two opening phrases of the *Tristan* prelude suggest A and C, which correspond to the overall tonal movement from A to C in the first act (Kindermann/Krebs 1996, 5). Bailey also demonstrated that nineteenth-century composers considered the major and minor forms of the key to be equivalents and interchangable (Bailey 1985, 116). From this perspective it is irrelevant that Bruckner's root motive suggests F minor, while the work concludes in F major. Other theorists have adapted Bailey's ideas and applied them, with great success, to other music of the nineteenth century, including mature works by Bruckner. It is, however, very surprising to find Bruckner employing tonal pairing in a small-scale, occasional work in 1854.

Vor Arneths Grab and the *Libera me* in F minor were written at the same time and share some musical material. Both works employ augmented sixths as dominant sevenths, and at least one passage seems to be a quotation from one piece to the other.

Example 2.13A:
Vor Arneths Grab—bars 15–16

Example 2.13B:
Libera me—bars 40–41

The title alone is likely to ensure that *Vor Arneths Grab* will remain something of a historical curiosity. This is unfortunate because the music, while simple, is captivating and reverberant. It also has a significant place in Bruckner's musical development and as such is essential to understanding his compositional evolution.

LAßT JUBELTÖNE LAUT ERKLINGEN—WAB 76

Written at the request of the primary choral society in Linz, the *Liedertafel* "*Frohsinn*,"[18] this short, celebratory chorus was performed April 22, 1854, at a reception in Linz for Elizabeth, bride-to-be of Habsburg Emperor, Franz Josef.[19] Sometime later it was slightly adapted to accommodate a new text, *Dir holde Heimat ...*, but this second version was not performed until after Bruckner's death,

---

[18]The *Liedertafeln* were male singing societies. The prototype was founded by Zelter in 1809, and took its name from the fact that its members first sat around a table and partook of refreshments. Such societies proliferated in the German-speaking countries during the nineteenth century (Apel 1972, 484).

[19]Franz Joseph and Elizabeth were married two days later on April 24, 1854, in the Augustinian church in Vienna.

and it does not appear that the composer had any hand in the adaption [20] (Göllerich/Auer 1974, III/1: 536–37).

At first glance it seems surprising that the major choral society based in a regional capital would engage a provincial monastery organist to provide a work for such a prestigious occasion. However, Bruckner was well known in Linz, having regularly visited to complete examinations in music and teaching. He also had a friend in the city who was influential in choral music performance. From October 1840 until July 1841, Bruckner attended the teacher-training school in Linz. His teacher of harmony and choral singing was August Dürrnberger (Göllerich/Auer 1974, I: 144–45). Dürrnberger remained a friend throughout Bruckner's years at St. Florian and played a major role in his eventual move to Linz as cathedral organist. Since Dürrnberger was involved with choral music in Linz, the request from the *Liedertafel "Frohsinn"* may well have originated with him.

Bruckner scored the work for male voices accompanied by an unusual brass ensemble of two trumpets, two horns, and *four* trombones (the score stipulates two bass trombones). Analysis of the brass writing reveals the reason for this particular instrumentation. While the horns and trumpets are used only to contribute brief fanfares, pedal tones, and occasionally the roots of otherwise incomplete chords, the trombones almost always double the voices. Four players were necessary to provide equal support for all choral lines.

Like many other works by this composer, including several investigated in this study, *Laßt Jubeltöne* ... begins with a distinctive motive that provides much of the ensuing musical material. Obvious derivatives of this motive form the beginning and the ending of each section, and all of the imitative passages are based on developments of it. Since no two statements of this tune are identical, it provides both musical unity and variety.

Example 2.14:
Laßt Jubeltöne ...—bars 1–4

---

[20]The revised version was performed in Vienna on June 15, 1898 (Grasberger 1977, 82), some twenty months after Bruckner's death. It seems likely that the new text was written for this performance.

One also wonders if the words were changed out of consideration for the Empress Elizabeth, who had been in constant mourning since the suicide of her son, Crown Prince Rudolf, in 1889. Under such circumstances, perhaps it was considered inappropriate to perform a celebratory work in which she was named. The new text takes a broader view, referring to God and Fatherland rather than to Franz Joseph and Elizabeth specifically. (Elizabeth herself was assassinated in Geneva less than three months later, on September 10, 1898.)

The structure of this passage is interesting for several reasons. The voices are in unison and sing what is essentially a fanfare. Harmony is provided by the brass instruments, especially the trombones. Choral fanfares will be encountered again, and this particular texture (unison voices with trombone harmony) has been observed earlier in this study.[21] However, this particular choral fanfare ends at its fourth bar with an upward leap of a minor seventh into dissonance—the voices sing E-flat against an incomplete B-flat dominant seventh chord in the brass. In effect, the voices create a chord in fifths that persists for a full two beats, before dissolving into the dominant seventh. This harmonic effect is heightened by the lack of a third in the underlying brass chord. The third, and the complete dominant seventh sonority, finally arrive when the voices resolve the E-flat to D. Such harmonic procedures are characteristic of this work. On-the-beat dissonance, often created by multiple suspensions, and unresolved seventh chords appear frequently, and add substantial expressiveness to the work as a whole. Also notable is the presence, perhaps for the first time, of the "Bruckner rhythm." This pattern, a duplet followed by a triplet or vice-versa, became a particular favourite of the composer and is considered to be one of his compositional fingerprints.

The work consists of two related sections (verses) followed by a brief coda. The sections are separated from each other by strong cadences in the tonic (E-flat major) and *fermatas*. Each verse reveals a similar mixture of homophonic and imitative passages; however, they also present substantial contrasts of harmony and texture. Verse one is harmonically straightforward, adhering almost exclusively to progressions that function tonally within the tonic—E-flat major. Verse two and the coda display a substantially enriched harmonic palette. Chromatic voice-leading creates chord progressions in thirds and many unexpected modulations—often to third-related keys. Verse one establishes the textural context of the piece. These ideas—homophony contrasted with polyphony, unison evolving into harmony, and pedal tones supporting streams of sixth chords—have been observed rather frequently in previously reviewed compositions. In verse two, these concepts are considerably developed. The homophony/polyphony contrast is sharpened by unaccompanied choral writing during the homophonic segments, and the imitative passages are intensified through the application of more complex contrapuntal devices. While verse one introduced two-voice canons, verse two presents double canons and a *fugato* in four voices. The "Bruckner rhythm," introduced in verse one, is a prominent musical element in verse two.

Laßt Jubeltöne ... is the first purely secular work to be examined, and it raises a problematic issue that characterizes much of Bruckner's non-sacred choral music. While the music itself is of substantial interest, the texts, which are often intensely patriotic, even jingoistic, are appropriate for very few performance situations. *Laßt Jubeltöne* ... contains an attractive blend of progressive harmony and timbral/textural variety, but it remains difficult to envision circumstances in which the work,

---

[21]See especially, verse three of *Psalm 114*.

with either of its texts, might be performed.

CANTATA: AUF, BRÜDER! AUF, UND DIE SAITEN ZUR HAND!—WAB 60

Arneth's successor as Prelate of St. Florian was Friedrich Mayr, who was installed on September 13, 1854. Since Mayr was musical, Bruckner was pleased about this appointment, and his most imposing work to date—the *Missa solemnis* in B-flat minor[22]—was written especially for the ceremony of installation (Göllerich/Auer 1974, II/1: 155). The following summer, to mark Mayr's nameday on July 17, 1855, he produced another impressive work, the *Cantata: Auf, Brüder! auf, und die Saiten zur Hand!*. In three movements it was scored for mixed choir, male choir, male quartet, two oboes, two bassoons, three horns, two trumpets, and three trombones—the largest ensemble employed in a wind work to this point in the composer's career.

Bruckner's utilization of these varied forces is interesting. The first movement employs men's chorus and the four soloists accompanied by horns and trombones. The second uses only unaccompanied male voices,[23] and the final movement incorporates most of the ensemble—mixed chorus, woodwinds, trumpets, trombones, and one solo horn. The diversity in scoring among the movements appears to have been inspired by the words. Since the text of the first verse expresses a male point of view, it was set for men's voices, accompanied by instruments that sound in a comparable register. The two lines of text used in movement two project a gentle, thoughtful mood. Thus, smaller forces and *a capella* timbre. The words of the final stanza are highly celebratory. Bruckner apparently wanted his music to represent the entire St. Florian community, so the choir was expanded to include female voices. It seems likely that the tessitura of the female choir necessitated the addition of oboes, while the inclusion of bassoons furnished a woodwind ensemble capable of four-part harmony, and allowed Bruckner to write rapid *arpeggiated,* scalic, or modulatory figures that would have been impossible on valveless brass instruments. The single horn plays frequently with the woodwinds, and also recalls horn motives from the first movement, providing a masterly stroke of musical unity. Trumpets were essential since this movement is filled with fanfares.

This *Cantata* is Bruckner's first extended composition for large wind ensemble and chorus. Remarkable in many ways, it demonstrates his gradual but inevitable progress toward a distinctive compositional "voice." Although the work does retreat to familiar territory from time to time, it also may be the first work in Bruckner's *oeuvre* where his personal style is clearly recognizable.

Like several other works in this study, the text was provided by the canon at

---

[22]Premiered on September 14, 1854 (Watson 1977, 141).

[23]The style of the music implies solo quartet, but the published score (in the *Collected Works*) specifies *Männerchor*.

St. Florian, Ernst Marinelli[24]:

Auf Brüder! auf, und die Saiten zur Hand!
Schon winket zärtlich die holde Camäne.
Sie rufet Euch in das herrliche Land
Lebendiger, ewig bezaubernder Töne,
Wir folgen, denn was sie uns singen he-
ißt,
Das lehrt uns ein liebend versöhnender
Geist.
Das strömt voll Jubel aus offener Kehle
Als träumt' es in Eden's Gefilden die
Seele.

Let's go, brothers! let's go and take the
strings into our hands!
The lovely Camäne is already waving
tenderly.
She is calling you into the great land
Of living and eternally enchanting tones,
We will follow for what she is asking us
to sing,
A loving, reconciliating spirit will teach
us.
This flows full of jubilation from an
open throat
As if the soul was dreaming it in the
fields of Eden.

Wohl ist's die Liebe, sie schlinget das
Band der Eintracht um Euch in heiliger
Schöne,
Wohlan so nahet und reichet ihr Pfand
dem Helden des Tages, Ihr würdigen
Söhne.

It is probably love, it ties the ribbon of
harmony around you in holy beauty,
Approach then and offer its pledge to the
hero of the day,
you worthy sons.

Heil, unserem Vater, den wir lieben, dem
das Herz in Freude schlägt,
Der von weiser Sorg' getrieben, seines
Hauses Lasten trägt.
Heil dem Förderer des Schönen, Heil
dem edelsten Mäcen,
Dem die Engel, die versöhnen, liebreich
mild zur Seite gehn.
Der das Schroffe weiß zu wenden und
der starren Form gebeut,
Der in seine Zeit zu senden weiß den
Blick, der uns erfreut:
Heil ihm dem Edlen, Kühnen, dessen
Kraft der Jungend gleich,
Dessen Herz an Liebe reich, dessen Herz
an Liebe reich.

Hail to our father whom we love, whose
heart is beating with happiness,
He who carries the burden of the house,
supported by his wise care.
Hail to the supporter of beauty, hail to
the most noble Maecenas,
At whose side, loving and mild, the
reconciling angels walk.
He who knows how to turn the roughness, and who commands the rigid form,
Who is able to send the glance that delights us:
Hail to him, the noble, brave, whose
strength is like that of youth
Whose heart is full of love, whose heart
is full of love.

(Göllerich/Auer 1974, II/1: 179–80)

(Translation by Ruth Thomas)

---

[24]In Marinelli's poem the term "Camäne" probably refers to the "Camenae"—the Muses of Art and Science in Roman mythology (Hamilton 1963, 46). "Maecenas" is undoubtedly Gaius Cilnius Maecenas (73?–78 B.C.), the Roman statesman who was the patron of Horace and Virgil, and, by extension, any patron of the arts.

As would many later compositions, movement one opens with a horn call. Bruckner repeated this particular call verbatim eight years later in his *Germanenzug*.[25]

Example 2.15:
Cantata: Auf, Brüder! ... Hand—bars 1–2

The call supplies much of the material for the entire work. For example, the first choral entry (bar 3) is a unison repeat of the horn call, harmonized at the cadence; then the call is restated by the horn while the other brass instruments provide the cadential harmony of the previous choral statement; the next choral passage (bar 7) duplicates the unison-to-harmony texture, but employs an inverted, then an augmented, version of the horn call. Similar permutations can easily be identified throughout all three movements.

This introduction is followed by a four-voice canon that would appear to be a pictorial realization of the words ("We will follow ... "). The canon dissolves into a passage in unison triplet rhythm that adheres closely to the natural cadence of the German language (Göllerich/Auer 1974, II/1: 180). The ensuing segment recalls plainchant, and the versicle/response procedures of liturgical performance. Although the choral responses largely comprise a single chord, chromatic inflections are introduced approaching the cadences, producing some very surprising sonorities, one of which duplicates the famous first chord of the *Scherzo* of *Symphony No. 9*[26] (Göllerich/Auer 1974, II/1: 180).

Example 2.16A:
Cantata: Auf, Brüder! ... Hand!—bars 21–22

---

[25]It occurs at the words "*die Freiheit, die Heimat*"—near the end of the third movement (Göllerich/Auer 1974, II/1: 180).

[26]In the Ninth Symphony this chord is startlingly dissonant because of its closed position voicing. In this work the dissonance is muted by open position scoring.

Example 2.16B:
Scherzo—Symphony No. 9—bar 3

p | (oboe and clarinets)

Overall, this short movement remains very close to the tonic (D major). However, Bruckner's use of both the major and minor forms of the submediant (B minor and B major) in the choral writing between bar seven and bar ten, and the Landini cadence that ends the movement provide delightful harmonic surprises. Also, throughout the movement he frequently uses the horns to echo the cadences of *a capella* choral passages. Such writing provides pleasing timbral variety and will be encountered again in later compositions.

Throughout the second movement the harmonic context is always clear. While the phrases display frequent contrapuntally created chords (some of which are very dissonant), the cadences are always conventional and in keys that are closely related to the tonic (G major). A great deal of expressiveness is contributed by unresolved seventh chords and on-the-beat dissonance, as well as uneven phrase length, much of which is generated through *fugato*. At bar 23–27 a descending chromatic bass line generates a stunning series of third-related chords.

Example 2.17:
Cantata: Auf Brüder! ... Hand!—Mvt. 2—bars 23–27

Em   GV7   CM   Em   Fr.6   DM?   AV7   F#o   GV7   CM   Am7

Two interesting examples of tone-painting also appear. The words, "it ties the ribbon of harmony around you," are set as a *fugato* in which the parts are intertwined, frequently crossing each other in register (Göllerich/Auer 1974, II/1: 181). The final section is a vocal fanfare. The words, "Approach then and offer its pledge to the hero of the day," clearly suggest a fanfare and anticipate those of the third movement. Since the fanfare modulates to D major, it prepares the final movement in both style and key.

Not surprisingly the celebratory third movement is full of trumpet fanfares. The first begins the movement and is an extension of the horn call that opened movement one. Its phrasing is unusual, consisting of three, three-bar phrases that firmly establish the tonic (D major).

Example 2.18:
Cantata: Auf, Brüder! ... Hand!—Mvt. 3—bars 1–9

It leads directly to the first choral entry (female voices), which appears abruptly in F-sharp major, at a *piano* dynamic and in a lyrical style. The words, "Our father, whom we love," obviously precipitated these changes, and the choir is accompanied by the woodwinds, which double choral lines and add a pulsating pedal point to energize the rhythm. The major mode fades into minor at the words "burden" and "care." Such melting of major into minor occurs frequently in this movement, and, while it has been observed in works previously addressed by this study, achieves a degree of subtlety not accomplished in earlier pieces. Bruckner would develop it to a high level in later compositions (Göllerich/Auer 1974, II/1: 182). The ensuing two choral passages (bar 18–32) show why the composer added woodwinds to the scoring. The music modulates from A major to F-sharp minor to E major to E minor to E major, and the surface rhythms become agitated. While brass instruments (especially those without valves) would be at a distinct disadvantage in this context, the woodwinds are able to double and ornament the vocal lines. In fact, the words, "he knows how to turn the roughness," assigned to basses alone, are enlivened by oboe *arpeggios*—a texture that Bruckner would return to frequently in the *E-minor Mass*.

At measure 41 a long section begins that uses only the last two lines of the poem. This music is very energetic, and employs a variety of imitative textures including two different *fugatos* that draw their subjects from material heard earlier in both this movement and the first movement. The tonality, while changing frequently, is always easily identifiable and, for the most part, remains close to the tonic (D major). F-sharp major and its accompanying fade to F-sharp minor are prominently featured.

Contrapuntal activity comes to an abrupt halt at bar 79. The coda that follows has several interesting features. During its first four bars, the female voices recall the tempo, style, and some of the content of the second movement. Its second section is the climax of the work and employs the entire ensemble. The bass line leaps a seventh, then descends through nearly two octaves in a curious mixture of whole- and half-steps that generate a truly astonishing sequence of third-related chords. Bruckner had never before created a passage of such compelling power. Following such harmonic intensity the unadorned plagal cadence sounds almost primordial in its simplicity (Göllerich/Auer 1974, II/1: 183). Bruckner assigns structural significance to these cadential bars by evoking the horn call from the beginning of the work.

Bruckner's effective use of the performing forces and close adherence to the text created a composition of considerable variety and drama. While much of the harmony is straightforward and the contrapuntal techniques familiar, this work represents a major step forward for this composer. A number of techniques that would become hallmarks of his later style appear here for the first time. Most important, the principle of cyclic form, which he probably drew from the music of Mendelssohn, is well developed in this work. Short passages of highly coloured chord progressions as well as distinctive longer-range tonal principles provide a glimpse of the harmonic imagination to come, and orchestrational ideas that would preoccupy him for many years appear, albeit in rudimentary form, for the first time in this *Cantata*. It may also be worth noting that the "Bruckner rhythm" subtly appears in the choral writing in both the first and second movements.

Chapter 3

Linz I: The Sechter Hiatus 1856–61

By the mid-1850s Bruckner's friends were urging him to leave the relative isolation of St. Florian and to find a position where his talents as a performer and composer could be recognized. Although he was frustrated by the low priority assigned to music, Bruckner was loath to abandon the security of the abbey for a much less certain career in music. However, a powerful impetus toward changing his situation came from a new source during the summer of 1855. Robert Führer, an organist from Prague, visited St. Florian and, after seeing the score of the *Missa solemnis*, suggested that Bruckner study theory and counterpoint with the eminent Viennese theorist and teacher Simon Sechter. Bruckner visited Sechter in July and was immediately accepted as a pupil. However, Sechter also advised him to look elsewhere for a position more suited to his musical talents. Having received this advice from such an august source, Bruckner secretly applied for the post of cathedral organist at Olomouc. This venture was disastrous. Not only did he not receive the appointment, but Prelate Mayr was furious when he heard about it and issued a sharp rebuke (Watson 1977, 12–13).

Thus, when the post of cathedral organist in Linz became available in the autumn of 1855, Bruckner did not apply. He did, however, travel to Linz on November 13 to hear the preliminary round of the competition. The result of this visit is the stuff of legend. When both of the applicants had played poorly, his friend August Dürrnberger approached him saying; "Tonerl,[1] you *must* play," then took him by the arm and escorted him to the organ loft. Bruckner performed brilliantly and won the preliminary competition. This time Mayr gave his blessing, even guaranteeing that Bruckner's position at St. Florian would be available should he choose to return within the next two years (Schönzeler 1970, 36). With the support

---

[1] The diminutive form of Anton in the Upper Austrian dialect (Watson 1977, 3), and a lifelong nickname.

of his superior, Bruckner went on to win the final examination and in late January 1856 was appointed cathedral organist in Linz (Watson 1977, 15–16). Now thirty-one years old, he was finally a full-time professional musician.

Some months previous to his application for the position in Linz, Bruckner embarked on a rigorous correspondence course in harmony and counterpoint with Sechter. Sechter based his teaching on Baroque and Classical models, and insisted that his students refrain from all free composition while studying with him (Simpson 1967, 12). That Bruckner took this directive seriously can be confirmed from his catalogue of works. Virtually no new compositions appeared during his apprenticeship to Sechter, 1855–61.[2] His lessons were carried out by correspondence, except for the periods of Advent and Lent when the organ was silent in the cathedral. During this time Bruckner had the permission of his new superior, Bishop Franz Joseph Rudigier, to travel to Vienna to spend six or seven weeks with Sechter (Watson 1977, 16–17).

Bruckner researchers have observed that Sechter's immutable rule regarding free composition and his pupil's unquestioning acceptance of it was probably a blessing in disguise. Bruckner's workload in Linz was staggering. In addition to his responsibilities at the cathedral, he was also organist in the *Pfarrkirche*, practiced organ several hours each day, took piano students, and became an active member of the *Liedertafel* "*Frohsinn*" (Cooke/Nowak 1985, 6–7). In later years Bruckner claimed that during these years he had spent seven hours a day on his exercises for Sechter (Doernberg 1960, 40). Considering the extent of his activities, it was probably to his advantage that he was prevented from engaging in extensive creative activities.[3]

Obviously, Bruckner's Sechter years are of limited interest from a compositional point of view. However, one work emerged during this time that has significance for this study.

CANTATA: AUF, BRÜDER! AUF ZUR FROHEN FEIER!—WAB 61

The music for this *cantata*, which used the text *Heil, Vater! ... Feste*, was written in St. Florian in 1852 to commemorate the nameday of Prelate Michael Arneth. When Bruckner moved to Linz in 1856, he maintained friendly relations

---

[2]There is evidence that this hiatus in compositional activity was at least partly self-imposed. Bruckner regarded the summer of 1863 as the beginning of his career as a professional composer, and considered all previous time to be his "study period." He restricted himself to exercises during this time, and stated that he would only begin to compose after his studies were completed (Hawkshaw 1984, 77).

[3]Robert Simpson has pointed out that, while few compositions appeared during the years of Bruckner's study with Sechter, we should not assume that he was creatively dormant. Bruckner was a master of improvisation at the organ. Simpson postulates that improvisation provided "solace and an outlet for his creative urges during this time of nearly seven years" (Simpson 1967, 15).

with his former employers. A year later he was asked to provide a work for the celebration of the nameday of Friedrich Mayr, Arneth's successor at St. Florian. This request caused him some difficulty. In 1857 he was immersed in his studies with Sechter, and was constrained by his teacher's prohibition against free composition. However, he was deeply appreciative of Mayr's support in the development of his career and evidently wanted to participate in the ceremony. His solution was to revive an earlier composition and adapt it to the situation at hand. Ernst Marinelli provided a new text, which Bruckner applied to his music by writing it directly onto the manuscript. The new version was performed on July 17, 1857, as an evening serenade in the garden of the abbey at St. Florian (Göllerich/Auer 1974, II/1: 112).

The texts for the 1852 and 1857 versions[4] have been confused in the Bruckner literature. Paul Hawkshaw has untangled the confusion, and the text quoted in its entirety below reflects his findings. Verse two, words and music, are crossed out of the autograph score with the new text, but do appear in the Collected Works edition.[5]

Auf, Brüder! auf zur frohen Feier!
Mit Festeskränzen schmückt die Leier,
Und innig wie's im Herzen schlägt.
Es weckt die Kraft der Lieder.
Der Tag, der seinen Namen trägt,
Kehrt uns gesegnet wieder.

Let's go, brothers! Let's go to the happy
celebration!
With festive wreaths decorate the lyre,
As it beats tenderly in the heart.
The power of the songs awakens.
The day which has his name
Returns to us in a blessed way.

Wo ist das Herz, das ihn nicht kennt,
Wo ist der Dank, der ihn nicht nennt,
In Liebe und Vertrauen?
Saht ihr wohl je auf Vater's Wort,
Auf solchen Freundes milden Hort,
getäuschte Hoffnung bauen?

Where is the heart that does not know
him,
Where is the thanks that does not name
him,
In Love and Trust?
Has anything built on our Father's word,
In such a friend's gentle refuge,
Ever betrayed our hope?

Nein, nein, die Hoffnung täuschet nicht,
Der Edle liebt der Liebe Pflicht,
Und wo der Vater streng gebeut
Ist auch der Freund zugleich bereit
Und knüpft das Band mit treuer Hand.

No, no, hope does not deceive,
The noble one loves the duty of love,
And where the father strictly orders
The friend at the same time is prepared
as well
To tie the ribbon with faithful hand.

Drum schlägt das Herz in froher Brust
Und folgt des Dankes hehre Lust
Auf seinen Lebenswegen.

Thus the heart beats in the happy breast
And follows the noble command of
thanks

---

[4] The 1852 version is discussed in detail in chapter two.

[5] See Hawkshaw 1984, 214–26.

Und droht die Zeit auch noch so schwer,	On his paths through life.
Es lächelt ihm von oben her	And even if times are threatening,
Der Segen.	The blessing smiles down on him from above.

O Herr im Himmel, siehe hier	O Lord in Heaven, look
Der Deinen Schar, die ruft zu dir.	Your flock calls upon you.
Und Preis und Dank ist ihr Gebet	And praise and thanks is their prayer
Und Segen, den sie heiß erfleht.	And blessing, which they earnestly implore.
Geliebt, geachtet und verehrt,	
Ist er auch deines Schutzes wert.	Loved, respected and worshipped,
	He also is worthy of your protection.

(Collected Works, 22/I/ No. 3b: 77–95, and Hawkshaw 1984, 216.)

(Translation by Ruth Thomas)

The new text precipitated a number of minor changes of rhythm and harmony, and other changes were made as well. The opening section of the first chorus was expanded from thirteen bars to fourteen, but the extra bar simply extended the cadence without altering the harmonic structure. In the 1852 version movements two and three were repeated as movements four and five. This repeat was eliminated from the second version, and the last half of movement two was re-composed.

These new bars stand in stark contrast to the rest of this composition and require additional comment. It would appear that Bruckner revisited them because of the change of text. In the 1852 version, the words "they were well sheltered" are set to a four-bar melody that is repeated and supported by a straightforward chord sequence in the tonic (G major). At this point in the 1857 revision, the words are "Ever betrayed our Hope? In such a friend's gentle refuge." The dramatic character of these phrases apparently drew Bruckner's attention, since the music he wrote for them displays a series of secondary seventh chords, chromatic voice-leading, multiple suspensions, and a prominent cadence in B major—the major form of the mediant of this key. These eight bars contrast sharply with the surrounding conservative context and provide a substantial performance challenge. Perhaps these considerations explain why this movement was crossed out of the autograph, and apparently was not included in the 1857 performance.

Like the original version, the revised score of this *cantata* is conventional in all musical aspects. Tonally conservative, accompanied choruses alternate with mildly chromatic, *a capella* movements for four male soloists. The instruments occasionally double the singers, but more frequently contribute brief introductions and endings, or simplified versions of choral lines. The new music written for movement two is the most interesting part of this score. The ideas displayed in these eight bars had become important considerations for Bruckner and are a clear illustration of his rapidly evolving compositional thinking during the 1850s.

Chapter 4

Linz II: "A Watchdog Unchained" 1861–68

At the end of March 1861, Bruckner concluded his studies with Sechter (Watson 1977, 17). He now knew everything about theory and counterpoint that could be taught to him, and, after nearly seven years of assignments and exercises, confessed to his friends that he felt "like a watchdog that has broken his chain" (Cooke/-Nowak 1985, 7). However, his "study period" was not quite completed. Always security-conscious, he applied for the diploma of the Vienna Conservatory, which would qualify him to teach harmony and counterpoint in conservatories of music. The exam was held on November 22, 1861, in the *Piaristenkirche* in Vienna, and led to Herbeck's[1] famous remark: "He should have examined us." (Watson 1977, 18, 142–3). He was now prepared to launch a career as a professional composer, and realized that he needed to broaden his interests to genres other than church music and male choruses. Orchestral music particularly beckoned. To this point Bruckner had written nothing for orchestra alone, and had produced few purely instrumental compositions. He felt inadequately prepared in the areas of form and orchestration, and turned to the Linz musician Otto Kitzler[2] for help (Schönzeler 1970, 43).

Kitzler's teaching methods were radically different from those of Sechter. A practicing musician, he based his teaching on the music of nineteenth-century

---

[1]Johann von Herbeck was a highly respected Viennese conductor and advocate of contemporary music—especially that of Bruckner and Liszt. Throughout the middle decades of the nineteenth-century, he conducted, at one time or another, all of the major musical organizations in the city, including the *Männergesang-Verein*, the *Singverein* of the *Gesellschaft der Musikfreunde*, the Philharmonic, and the Court Opera. He died in 1877 (Sadie 1988, 337).

[2]Kitzler was the principal cellist and occasionally the conductor of the Linz Municipal Theatre (Cooke/Nowak 1985, 9).

masters, particularly Beethoven and Mendelssohn[3] (Cooke/Nowak 1985, 9).
Exercises and compositions written during this time are preserved in what Hawkshaw calls the *Kitzler Studienbuch*, and show that Bruckner's studies began before
Christmas 1861 and lasted until July 1863. Unlike Sechter, Kitzler apparently
encouraged composition. This volume contains twenty-five completed pieces,
although these were obviously exercises and not intended for performance. The
folio also shows that Kitzler led his student systematically through the small
musical forms to the large forms and then to the orchestration of previously written
and new compositions (Hawkshaw 1984, 84–102).

While Kitzler's carefully structured tuition undoubtedly benefited Bruckner,
the most lasting impact on the composer came from quite a different source. In late
1862 Kitzler decided to mount the first performance in Linz of Wagner's *Tannhäuser*, and invited Bruckner to study the score with him. This score and the performance on February 13, 1863, were a turning point in Bruckner's development
(Cooke/Nowak 1985, 10):

[Bruckner] had spent his years in unquestioned dependence on established authority and in
the exploration of what was deemed permissible on music paper. In Wagner's score he found
music which went beyond all his previous experience, and yet what he heard convinced him.
... Wagner's music led him to the simple conclusion that Wagner was, no doubt, an "authority", a "Master". And so it was with the precept and the example of a "Master" that Bruckner
flung open the door to creative freedom. (Doernberg 1960, 44–5)

Within little more than a year after the *Tannhäuser* performance, Bruckner had
produced the *Mass in D Minor*—a work of astonishing individuality in form,
harmony, and melodic structure.[4] In this composition the second Bruckner—the
Bruckner for the ages—manifests, seemingly without warning. The composer himself never discussed the transformation of his approach, except to comment regarding the innovative style of his new Mass: "I didn't dare before" (Schönzeler
1970, 45). With Wagner as his new mentor, Bruckner stood on the threshold of a
career that would ultimately identify him with compositional invention and surround him with controversy.

While the transformation of his style was unquestionably abrupt and compre-
hensive, Bruckner's works contained hints of it from the very beginning. Researchers investigating the pre-1863 works noted brief passages in many of them that

---

[3]Bruckner had encountered Mendelssohn's music in 1847 when he heard a performance
of *St. Paul* in Linz. The music impressed him deeply, and Mendelssohn's influence can easily
be heard in many subsequent works. By 1853 his friend, Schaarschmidt, felt obligated to
warn him about his reliance on Mendelssohn as a model and to encourage him to look
instead to the music of J. S. Bach (Watson 1977, 9, 11–12).

[4]The individuality of this work is especially notable. Doernberg points out that it contains
"no more than a passing trace of Wagnerian influence" (Doernberg 1960, 45), a view that
is supported by other researchers (see Cooke/Nowak 1985, 38–39).

sounded like Wagner, even though Bruckner was not exposed to this composer's music until Kitzler introduced him to *Tannhäuser* in late 1862.[5] Virtually all of the compositions reviewed in this study display instances of strikingly original harmony that, while not necessarily Wagnerian, illustrate a vital and unconventional harmonic imagination. Unlike Wagner and Liszt, Bruckner apparently did not see himself as a revolutionary whose purpose was to rewrite the theory texts and establish a new approach to composition. He seems, instead, to have been a natural free thinker whose ideas absorbed all conventional approaches and then moved beyond them in an organic process of evolution. His introduction to Wagner's music simply provided him with a broader framework in which to exercise his copious gifts of invention.

The post-Sechter years in Linz were a period of immense importance for Bruckner. Not only did he initiate his new style, but he also produced some of his most enduring compositions (especially the three masses in D minor, E minor, and F minor, written in 1864, 1866, and 1867–68, respectively). He also began to establish himself as a composer of symphonic music—a genre that would preoccupy him for the rest of his life and would include his most significant contributions to the musical literature. From the point of view of this study, these years are also very important. During this time Bruckner composed six impressive works for winds, several of which are among the most significant ever written for the medium.

AFFERENTUR REGI—WAB 1

An Offertory, *Afferentur regi*, was completed on November 7, 1861, and first performed in St. Florian on December 13 of the same year (Grasberger 1977, 5). Bruckner's studies with Sechter had concluded in the spring of 1861, and this short work was among the first compositions produced after the lifting of his teacher's prohibition on free composition. All of the works of this time are polyphonic, almost as if Bruckner was flaunting his newly acquired contrapuntal virtuosity.

The manuscript sources and the scoring of this piece have generated considerable difference of opinion in the literature. No authenticated manuscript exists for the best-known version of this work, the setting for chorus and three trombones. However, the archives of the monastery at Kremsmünster hold an autograph, unquestionably genuine, that is scored for *a capella* choir. The existence of this manuscript has lead researchers to assume that Bruckner composed two versions of *Afferentur regi*, one for choir alone and a second for choir with trombone accompaniment. Paul Hawkshaw has carefully investigated the composer's working methods during the 1850s and 1860s, and takes a different view. He points out that, when composing his small-scale liturgical pieces for voices and trombones, Bruckner usually wrote out the voice parts first and added the instruments later. He

---

[5]See Schönzeler 1970, 43–45; Watson 1977, 19–20; and many places in Göllerich and Auer.

contends that the Kremsmünster manuscript is working copy, not a separate version of the work (Hawkshaw 1984, 151–54). If one accepts Hawkshaw's view—and his arguments are convincing—there never was more than a single version of this piece.

Words and music provide a clear insight into the genesis of this composition. The text is the Offertory of the first Common Mass for a Virgin Martyr (*Liber Usualis* 1952, 1215–20),[6] and December 13, the day on which this work was premiered, is the feast day of St. Lucy (Virgin and Martyr) for which this Offertory is specified in the liturgy (*Liber Usualis* 1952, 1322–25). Bruckner undoubtedly composed his setting for the celebration, at St. Florian, of the feast day of St. Lucy. The music provides further confirmation. The initial motive of the work is derived from the plainchant associated with this particular Offertory—a chant that would have been well known to the residents of St. Florian.

Structurally, the work is a simple A-B-A$_1$. The initial A consists of two statements of the same four-voice *fugato*, the subject of which is based on plainchant. Bruckner apparently was intrigued by the wide skips in the fourth phrase of the chant, and built the initial motive of his setting from this phrase.

Example 4.1A:
Liber Usualis, p. 1219—*Afferentur*—4th phrase

Example 4.1B:
Afferentur regi—bars 1–7

Although the key signature and the first two notes (C and F) suggest F major, no firm key is established during the initial few bars. The harmony is modal rather than tonal, and lacks any strong dominant sonorities. Even the V^7 → I progression in B-flat major at bar 5–6 is weakened by a hesitation on the bar-line between the

---

[6]The text is: Afferentur regi virgines post eam: proximae ejus afferentur tibi in laetitia et exsultatione: adducentur in templum regi Domino. [The king's daughter is led before the king, with bridesmaids in her train. Her ladies-in-waiting follow and enter the king's palace with gladness and rejoicing (Proffitt 1991, 9)]. These words also make up most of verses 14–15 of *Psalm 45.*

two chords. The first clear cadence occurs at bar 7—a plagal cadence in D minor. Even here, however, the sub-dominant chord is minor, leaving the sense of resolution to be established largely through rhythm. The second statement of the *fugato* is slightly altered, and transposed down a minor third. However, by its sixth bar it has returned to its original pitch level, and is extended to cadence in A major. The ensuing B section consists of a stream of sixth chords over a pedal A. Such structures, reminiscent of *fauxbourdon*, were particularly favoured by Bruckner and have been noted frequently in this study. The final A_1 section begins exactly like the opening except that the trombones double the first three entries of the *fugato*. This section is chromatic but the harmony functions tonally within F major. The closing bars are interesting. Essentially a simple ii → V^7 → I cadence in F major, the entire progression is suspended over a tonic pedal creating a striking effect that Göllerich and Auer describe as "soothing and at the same time transfiguring, like an organ postlude" (Göllerich/Auer 1974, III/1: 123).

The trombones are used sparingly and are marked optional in the score. Their primary purpose is to guide the pitch of the choir during the modulations, but, since this piece was written for a specific religious ceremony, Bruckner may also have included them because of their liturgical connotations. This work, however, is easily performable without them.

Musically, *Afferentur regi* seems poised between Bruckner's two styles. The complexity and natural flow of the counterpoint demonstrates the degree to which he had absorbed Sechter's teaching, but the harmony, particularly that of the closing section, harkens back to the early 1850s. Despite the assuredness of the writing, this work displays more stylistic affinity with earlier compositions than with those yet to come. Considering its chronology and origin, this is hardly surprising. Serene and brief, it reveals a confident, highly skilled composer, but provides little indication of the upheaval that was soon to impose itself on his thinking and change his music forever.

FESTCANTATA: PREISET DEN HERRN—WAB 16

Throughout his career in Upper Austria, Bruckner was consistently supported by influential religious leaders. In St. Florian the Prelates Arneth and Mayr were his benefactors, and in Linz, Bishop Franz Joseph Rudigier took up the role of advocate and friend. A number of Bruckner's works from this period were initiated by Rudigier, including this *Festcantata*.

In 1854 Pope Pius IX had proclaimed the doctrine of Mary's Immaculate Conception. In response to his Pope's decree, Rudigier marshalled the energies of his diocese to the construction of a new cathedral in Linz that would venerate this dogma. A project of such magnitude required a sustained effort over a long period of time, but by the spring of 1862 the foundations were in place. The cornerstone was dedicated on May 1, 1862, and for this celebration Rudigier asked Bruckner to compose a large-scale festive cantata (Göllerich/Auer 1974, II/1: 134–35). Completed on April 25, the work was scored for male chorus and large wind orchestra.[7] The outdoor performance venue dictated the choice of wind instruments, but the reasoning behind Bruckner's decision to use only male voices is less obvious. Perhaps he was influenced by the popular nineteenth-century Germanic tradition of combining *Männergesang-Vereinen* with military bands for outdoor ceremonies. Also, it should be noted that he was the conductor of the *Liedertafel "Frohsinn"* from November 1860 until September 1861 (Watson 1977, 142), and that this choir participated in the premiere[8] (Grasberger 1977, 20).

The text was written especially for the event by Professor Dr. Pamesberger, and was printed and distributed to all present at the ceremony[9] (Göllerich/Auer 1974, III/1: 135). Apparently, everyone was expected to participate. However, since the music was newly written, it is difficult to imagine how this would have been possible in any of the movements except the chorale, *"Des Landes Stämme ..., "* which may have been familiar to many in the audience:

Preiset den Herrn,   Praise the Lord,
Lobsingt seinem heiligen Namen!   Sing praises to His holy name!

Grund und Eckstein bist du, Herr,   Base and cornerstone are you, Lord,
Deiner Kirche groß und hehr.   (For) your great and exalted church.

Taue deine Kraft und Stärke   Spread your power and strength
Über Fundament und Stein,   Over foundation and stone,
Die wir zu dem heil'gen Werke   That we for your holy work
Weihend senken ein.   Consecrate one planting.

Preiset den Herrn, Maria preiset,   Praise the Lord, praise Mary,

---

[7]The score calls for: two flutes, two oboes, two clarinets in D, two clarinets in A, two bassoons, two horns in G, two horns in D, three trumpets in D, three trombones, tuba, and timpani.

Bruckner had not previously written for such an ensemble, and one wonders if Kitzler influenced this instrumentation. Orchestration was one of the primary focuses of Bruckner's studies at this time, and it seems hardly coincidental that, with the exception of the extra pair of clarinets, the instrumentation of this work duplicates almost exactly the wind section that he would use for his first six symphonies. [He expanded the trumpet section from two to three for *Symphony No. 3*, and added tuba for the first time in *Symphony No. 4.* Cooke/-Nowak 1985, 46–47)]. There can be no doubt that he consulted with his teacher during the composition of this piece. One of the autograph sketches contains pencilled annotations in a hand that has been identified as that of Kitzler (Hawkshaw 1984, 55–56).

[8]The performance was conducted by the composer and teacher, Engelbert Lanz (Grasberger 1977, 20). Lanz was the choirmaster of the *Liedertafel "Frohsinn,"* and composed an eight-voice offertory *Misit Dominus* especially for this event (Obermayer-Marnach 1972, 21).

[9]The versification of Pamesberger's poem has been altered below, in order to reflect how Bruckner divided it in his setting.

Ohne Makel empfangen!

Aus der Erde Schoß
Wächst der Bau
Riesengroß
In des Himmels Blau.

Das ist der Unbefleckten Haus,
Drin öffnet sich die Gnadenquelle,
Und strömet reich und helle
Ins Land hinaus.

Des Landes Stämme wallen fromm
Aus allen Gauen zu dem Dom
Von unsrer lieben Frauen;
Sie grußen sie viel tausendmal
Und finden Heil im Gnadensaal
Durch Glauben und Vertrauen.

Preiset den Herrn,
Lobsingt seinem heiligen Namen,
Maria preiset,
Die mächtige Helferin, Amen.

(Collected Works, 22/II/No. 6: 147–77;
and Göllerich/Auer 1974, III/1: 135–36)

Who immaculately conceived!

From the earth's womb
Sprouts this great building
Rising into the blue Heavens.

This is the house of the Immaculate,
Which reveals for you the spring of mercy inside,
And streams richly bright
Into the land beyond.

The country tribes flow piously
From all districts toward the cathedral
Of our lovely women;
They greet her many thousand times
And find salvation in mercy's hall
Through faith and trust.

Praise the Lord,
Sing praises to His holy name,
Praise Mary,
The Almighty helper, Amen.

(Translation by Ruth Thomas)

This composition is a clear development on Bruckner's earlier works in this genre. Cast in eight short movements, it is musically integrated through the repetition of motives and textures, and by close thematic relationships among the movements. While these principles have been observed in earlier works, their use is substantially enhanced in this *Festcantata*. Like the *Cantata: Auf, Brüder! auf... Hand* of 1855, this work demonstrates Bruckner's interest in timbrally contrasted movements, but here the range of tone colour contrast is considerably widened.

Melodically, this composition draws on Mendelssohn's *Symphony No. 2, op. 52*. Kitzler admired Mendelssohn's music and incorporated it into his teaching. However, these two works have another, more fundamental, connection. The fourth movement of Mendelssohn's second symphony is a *cantata*, *Lobgesang*, which uses a number of textual phrases that are very similar to those being set by Bruckner. Considering the "organic" connection between the texts and Kitzler's partiality to Mendelssohn's music, it is apparent that Bruckner looked to this symphony as a model when composing a similar work.

The first movement opens with a distinctive unison motive in the winds that comprises a descending octave and a dotted rhythm. When the choir responds in the second bar, the motive is harmonized. Such openings can be found in Bruckner's works of all periods. The third and fourth bars are a quotation of the first two bars of the *Cantata: Heil, Vater! ... Feste* from 1852.

Example 4.2A:
Preiset den Herrn—bars 1–4

Example 4.2B:
Heil, Vater! ... Feste—bars 1–2

The remainder of the opening section is a development of the *Heil, Vater!* motive in a homophonic texture that initially uses only the tonic triad (D major) then cadences on the dominant. The distinctiveness of these opening bars is important, since Bruckner repeats them in movements four and eight in order to provide musical unity. The second section of this movement provides textural and harmonic contrast. The voices present a two-voice canon at the third that rises sequentially and is supported by a pulsing eighth-note accompaniment. This music is suddenly in B minor. The final few bars return to the homophonic texture and the key of the beginning of the movement.

Movement two follows without pause. The initial part of this movement is a four-voice *fugue* exposition complete with countersubject and related free material. Although the contrapuntal writing is conventional, the harmonic context is far from orthodox. The movement begins in B minor (which explains the abrupt turn to this key in the initial movement), and the first two entries are as expected—the first statement in the tonic followed by a real answer on the dominant (F-sharp). However, when the next pair of entries occur, the music jumps suddenly to D major with the subject appearing on the tonic and dominant of the new key. Nor does this conclude the interesting harmonic twists. The *fugue* exposition ends abruptly in a series of *sforzando* chords that briefly establish F-sharp major, then the key fades to F-sharp minor. Precisely this fade was noted in the analysis of the *Cantata: Auf, Brüder! auf... Hand,* and it will be seen again in later works. This movement concludes with a typical Brucknerian extended cadence. A towering unison C-sharp and D appear in measure 46–47, followed by a conventionally harmonized cadence in F-sharp minor.

The *fugue* subject connects this movement to the previous one through its use of a descending octave, and includes the first obvious reference to Mendelssohn. Its last half is a quotation of a fragment from the main theme of that composer's *Symphony No. 2*.

Example 4.3A:
Preiset den Herrn—fugue subject

Example 4.3B:
Mendelssohn—*Symphony No. 2*—main theme

The third movement also displays a number of interesting features. Structurally, it consists of a chorale with two timbrally contrasted statements of the same verse. The initial statement is scored for solo male quartet, while the second incorporates the full chorus plus an accompanying melodic strand, first in two (flute, clarinet), then in three (flute, clarinet, bassoon), solo woodwinds. The woodwinds present a single line in octaves that consists of scales or *arpeggios* extracted from the underlying harmony. The eighth-note figuration adds substantial rhythmic momentum to the texture, and is reminiscent of similar structures in the final movement of the *Cantata: Auf, Brüder! auf... Hand*, and in the *E-minor Mass*.

Harmonically, this movement is also interesting. The key is A major despite the key signature of two sharps, and the modulation from the previous movement is accomplished in a particularly striking way. Movement two cadences in F-sharp minor. Movement three begins on a V^7/V chord (BV^7) in the new key (A major) that is created through common tones in two voices, and whole-step and minor third movement in the others. This chord progresses through a leading tone seventh to the new tonic (A major).

Example 4.4:
Preiset den Herrn—Mvt. 2, bar 26—Mvt. 3, bars 1–3

In effect, this series of chords is a circle-of-fifths progression (F♯m → BV⁷ → G♯°⁷ [EV⁷] → AM → EV⁷ → AM), and may imply that these two movements be performed without pause.[10] Unquestionably, the words support this contention. In his setting Bruckner divided the second stanza of Pamesberger's poem between movements two and three. Linking these movements in performance would provide a significantly stronger realization of the text.

This surprising progression is complimented throughout the movement by a considerable amount of chromatic voice-leading and third-related modulation. Both statements modulate to F-sharp minor, but, while the first returns to the tonic (A major), the end of the second is recomposed in order to conclude in F-sharp major.[11] This recomposition apparently was necessary to prepare the new key in movement four—D major. The descent of a major third between tonalities was particularly favoured by Bruckner (Simpson 1967, 168), and was developed to a high degree in his symphonies.

Movement four begins by recalling the distinctive music that opened this composition. However, only the first five bars are exactly restated. The rest of the movement consists of two new musical ideas. This new music was precipitated by the words, which address Mary and the Immaculate Conception for the first time. Both of these themes, central to the concept and purpose of this work, are represented by unique and aurally identifiable music. The music associated with the Immaculate Conception consists of a series of first- and second-inversion chords over a dominant pedal, similar to the B section of *Afferentur regi*. "Mary's music" is drawn directly from the first four bars of the piece (see Example 4.2A), but is recomposed into an easily recognizable texture.

Example 4.5:
Preiset den Herrn—Mvt. 4, bars 18–22

The fifth movement is brief, only nine bars long, but presents some of the most remarkable music seen thus far in this work. Scored for solo bass with a simple accompaniment, its melodic and harmonic structures anticipate future develop-

---

[10]A similar progression appears between movements one and two of *Germanenzug*, and almost certainly implies that the movements be bridged in performance.

[11]Both of these keys, F-sharp minor and F-sharp major, were important secondary tonalities in the previous movement. The recalling of secondary keys from previous movements occurs frequently in this work, and is an important integrating element.

ments in Bruckner's style. The bass solo consists of two phrases, both of which incorporate an extensive range—a compound diminished fifth in each case. The total compass required is a compound minor sixth.[12] At the climax of the movement, the soloist is required to leap downward by a compound minor third. Bruckner would create similar dramatic melodic contours frequently in later works, notably in the main theme of *Symphony No. 7*. In this instance the huge melodic curve is an example of tone painting. The words describe the cathedral growing out of the ground to reach high into the sky. The music inscribes a tall arch reflecting the Gothic style of the building.

Harmonically, this movement is also quite surprising. It begins in G major, and the first five bars are harmonized by common chords within that key. However, beginning at bar six a chromatically ascending soprano line and a chromatically descending bass line combine to generate a series of chords that reach well outside the confines of the tonality, and are difficult to explain by traditional root-progression analysis. The final cadence is also remarkable. An augmented sixth in C major is substituted for the dominant of G, a progression that appears frequently in Bruckner's later works.

Example 4.6:
***Preiset den Herrn*—Mvt. 5, bars 6–9 (harmony only)**

Movement five ends in G major, which sets up another descent by a major third to the key of the sixth movement—E-flat major. This movement, scored for male quartet with the first tenor serving as soloist, contains some of the most appealing music in the entire work. Structured in two similar but not identical verses, this gentle and expressive music seems an apt reflection of the words, which are a meditation on the Immaculate Conception. The first verse is harmonically complex. Chromatic voice-leading often generates chords that cannot be identified within a tonally functional frame, and can only be understood through linear rather than harmonic analysis. Interestingly, this verse ends in the dominant (B-flat major) with the same progression that concluded movement five—augmented (German) sixth → tonic—but in this case the cadence is elaborated contrapuntally so that the voices resolve at different times. The second verse is somewhat more tonally functional, but passes through F minor and A-flat major

---

[12]Bruckner probably wrote it for the outstanding bass, Karl Weilnböck (Göllerich/Auer 1974, III/1: 138).

before cadencing in the tonic.

Example 4.7:
Preiset den Herrn—Mvt. 6, bars 14–16

The primary motive, stated at the beginning of each verse by the soloist alone, is related to preceding melodic ideas through its dotted rhythm, but is also a development of the main theme of Mendelssohn's *Symphony No. 2*. A reference to this theme was previously heard in the *fugue* subject of the second movement.

Example 4.8A:
Preiset den Herrn—Mvt. 6, bars 1–5

Example 4.8B:
Mendelssohn—*Symphony No. 2*—bars 1–3

An interesting contrapuntal device appearing in the third bar has the second tenor repeating the primary motive exactly, while the first tenor adds a type of descant above. No similar passage has been observed in the works reviewed by this study.

Movement six is followed by a brief interlude for clarinets and bassoons that is labelled "*Praeludium*" in the score. The primary purpose of these ten bars is to modulate from E-flat major to G major in preparation for the ensuing chorale. In effect, these bars function as a miniature chorale prelude, and the title ascribed to them would seem to confirm that Bruckner intended them for precisely this purpose.

The next movement is the chorale "*Des Landes Stämme* ...," stated very simply and without accompaniment. Bruckner's harmonization is functionally diatonic within G major, but does cadence on both the mediant and the submediant. Göllerich and Auer point to the incongruity of a German Protestant chorale appearing in a work dedicated to Roman Catholic dogma, specifically Mary and the Immaculate Conception, neither of which have as central a place in Protestant doctrine. However, Bruckner had become familiar with Lutheran chorales through his study of the music of J. S. Bach (Watson 1977, 73) and had always been interested in them.[13] The brass chorale was to become a significant aspect of his symphonic style (Göllerich/Auer 1974, III/1: 193). Also, his casual regard for the texts of works without a specific liturgical function is well documented.[14] Apparently, Bruckner felt that this particular chorale suited his musical purposes, and its source was irrelevant to him.[15]

The finale is by far the longest and most complex of all the movements. Since this work is primarily dedicated to Mary, Bruckner chose to emphasize the words referring to her throughout this section. The music reflects this choice. Much of this movement consists of restatements of, or variations on, the motive associated with Mary that was introduced in movement four. However, music from earlier movements is recalled in other ways as well.

The final movement begins by restating the first nineteen bars of the piece. In the initial movement, Bruckner followed these measures with an extended cadence in the tonic that employed a series of secondary dominant progressions. Here, however, the cadence is simplified and modulates to the dominant[16] (A major) in order to prepare a dramatic change of texture that is unlike anything else in this work. The forward momentum of the music seems to hesitate. The dynamic level drops from *fortissimo* to *mezzo-forte*, the choral parts suddenly become unison, and a new counterpoint appears in clarinets and bassoons. Since this new contrapuntal line is largely scalar and employs woodwinds, this striking passage would seem to be a timbral recall of the second half of movement three. The text is "*Maria preiset*" and the unison choral line is a development of "Mary's motive" (see Example 4.5). Four bars later the music begins regathering momentum. At the words "*die mächtige Helferin,*" harmony is reestablished in the choral writing, and

---

[13]See, for example, his settings of *In jener letzten der Nächte* of 1848, and *Dir, Herr, dir will ich mich ergeben* of 1858 (Cooke/Nowak 1985, 58).

[14]His secular compositions often use decidedly mediocre poetry. Also informative in this regard is an incident that occurred after he first heard *Die Walküre*. At the conclusion of the opera, he reportedly asked someone: "Tell me, why did they burn the woman at the end?" (Schönzeler 1970, 46). Apparently he was totally engrossed in the music and had completely lost any sense of the plot.

[15]One should also note that a similar unaccompanied chorale appears during the "*Lobgesang*" *cantata* in Mendelssohn's second symphony.

[16]Melodically, these bars contain a subtle reference to the first two bars of the third movement.

Bruckner creates another variation on the music associated with Mary.

Example 4.9:
Preiset den Herrn—Mvt. 8, bars 23–25

Example 4.10:
Preiset den Herrn—Mvt. 8, bars 30–32

Another clever compositional device appears in the final measures. The motive identified with God from the first bars of the work and a hint of "Mary's music" are combined in counterpoint. The intention is clearly poetic. Bruckner has created a musical illustration of the symbiotic relationship between God and Mary that is spelled out in the text. The work concludes with a simple plagal cadence in D major.

Example 4.11:
Preiset den Herrn—concluding bars

Preiset den Herrn is an important contribution to the repertoire for chorus and winds, and demonstrates Bruckner's primary concerns at the time of its composition—form and orchestration. His interest in form is reflected in the closely related melodies, repetition of motives among the movements, and especially in the finale, which sums up the entire composition by making reference to much of what has preceded it. These techniques give the work a sense of unity and completeness that is often missing in the work of lesser composers, and would become permanent parts of Bruckner's working methods. Kitzler's teachings on orchestration are obvious in the imaginative use of the performing forces. The contrast of full ensemble with a variety of smaller groups is convincing, and Bruckner has made effective use of the timbral resources available to him.

This composer's contrapuntal skills and harmonic imagination are also apparent. A wide variety of homophonic and polyphonic textures appear, and the counterpoint generates considerable drama. Harmonically, most of this work can be analyzed using the traditional techniques of functional harmony. However, these procedures break down when faced with unprepared modulations and highly chromatic voice-leading. Especially in the two unaccompanied quartets,[17] Bruckner's chord and key choices are often surprising and indicate that he was developing much more confidence in his unorthodox harmonic ideas. He was finally ready to hear Wagner's music.

GERMANENZUG—WAB 70

Germanenzug occupies a place of immense importance in Bruckner's compositional evolution. The composer considered this secular cantata to be his "first real composition"; that is, it was the first work written after he had completed his "study period."[18] It was also his first composition to be published, and, during his lifetime, was among his most frequently performed pieces. He certainly took its creation very seriously. Between July 1863 and late summer 1864, he produced no fewer than four different versions, focussing on this work to the virtual exclusion of all other composition[19] (Hawkshaw 1990, 21, 26–29). He was especially fond of the second movement ("In Odin's Hallen ist es licht"), and requested that it be performed at his funeral. When the time came, his request was honoured by the Academic Choral Society of Vienna and a horn quartet from the Court Opera ("Anton Bruckner" 1896, 4).

The genesis of this work is rather complicated. In June 1863 the Linzer Zeitung announced that a composition competition would be part of the first Oberösterreichisches Sängerfest, scheduled for August 14–15, 1864, in Linz. Bruckner originally intended to submit a revised version of an earlier work, Zigeuner-Waldlied, to this contest, but decided that the text, a gypsy forest song, was inappropriate for a festival of male choruses. He approached the poet August Silberstein for a more suitable text. However, when he received Silberstein's poem, he realized that the music for Zigeuner-Waldlied, which was in 3/4 meter, would not fit the new words with their images of marching warriors and epic battles. He composed a new piece, in 4/4 meter, drawing material from his earlier composition

---

[17]Apparently the Liedertafel "Frohsinn" was expanded with "invited guest singers and students" for the first performance (Göllerich/Auer 1974, III/1: 135). This may explain the contrast in difficulty between these quartet movements and the choruses.

[18]His studies with Kitzler concluded on July 10, 1863 (Hawkshaw 1990, 28).

[19]Between September 1863 and June 1864, Bruckner produced only three short pieces: Stille Betrachtung an einem Herbstabend, Herbstlied, and Um Mitternacht.

(Hawkshaw 1990, 21–22, 28).

This, at least, is the generally accepted view. Two letters—one from Silberstein to Bruckner dated July 27, 1863, and a response from the composer two days later—are usually quoted as evidence for this chain of events. Silberstein's letter simply accompanied the poem and made a few compositional suggestions. Bruckner's is more interesting:

What do you, Sir, advise me to do regarding the rhythm? I can probably keep my old three-part rhythm (3/4 meter) or am I supposed to, or do I even have to, use the two-part rhythm for marches (4/4 meter) in order to do justice to the poem, and it is, after all, called *Germanenzug*, "The Germanic people stride ... " etc., this gives me a headache....
...I repeat my thanks as well as my urgent request for your opinion regarding the rhythm (if the *Zigeuner-Waldlied* etc. was suitable in the three-part). (Göllerich/Auer 1974, III/1: 206)

Silberstein's response, if he made one, is unrecorded, and, since no score of the *Zigeuner-Waldlied* survives, it is impossible to know how it may have influenced *Germanenzug*, or if the accepted sequence of events is accurate. Bruckner obviously decided that, for *Germanenzug,* 4/4 was the proper meter. None of the surviving sketches contain any music in 3/4 time (Hawkshaw 1990, 21–22).

Bruckner apparently had the first version completed by September 1, 1863, because he mentioned it in a letter to Rudolf Weinwurm[20] (Hawkshaw 1990, 21). However, the autumn of 1863 and the early winter of 1864 brought several developments that drew his attention back to this piece. The festival, initially a local event, gradually took on a much broader scope that included much of Austria, and, sometime during these months, the publisher Josef Kränzl and the festival committee agreed that the winning compositions would be published. On January 10, 1864, the competition jury announced eight winning titles, including *Germanenzug*. Since it was now clear that this work was to be his first publication, Bruckner had a strong incentive to ensure that it was as close as possible to his conception, and that the edition be free of mistakes. Between January 1864 and the late summer or autumn of that year when the first published edition was released, Bruckner produced at least three additional versions of the *cantata* (Hawkshaw 1990, 22, 26, 28–29).

During the spring of 1864, the festival was postponed. It was rescheduled for June 4–6, 1865, and renamed the *Oberösterreichisches-Salzburgisches Sänger-bundesfest* (Hawkshaw 1990, 30). At the festival the *Liedertafel "Frohsinn,"* conducted by Bruckner, presented the first performance of *Germanenzug* on June 5 (Grasberger 1977, 76). It had been awarded second prize[21] in the composition competition, a fact that caused Bruckner much displeasure (Göllerich/Auer 1974,

---

[20]Weinwurm was a close friend of Bruckner during his Linz years. His assistance was crucial in facilitating Bruckner's eventual move to Vienna (Watson 1977, 165–66).

[21]The winning composition was *Germania* by Rudolf Weinwurm (Hawkshaw 1990, 29).

III/1: 319).

Silberstein's text deals with Teutonic mythology, the same stories that Wagner was to use in his *Der Ring des Nibelungen*:

Germanen durchschreiten des Urwaldes Nacht,
sie ziehen zum Kampfe, zu heiliger Schlact.
Es stehen die Eichen im düsteren Kreis,
und sie rauschen so bang, und flüstern so leis,
als sollte der Krieger gewaltigen Schwarm
durchdringen die Ahnung, erfassen der Harm!
Sie aber, sie wandeln urkräftigen Tritt's
so nahet der Donner mit zündendem Blitz!
Und aus des Gezweiges wild düsterem Hang
da wird es jetzt lauter, da tönt ein Gesang,
denn der Walkyren bewachend Geleit
umschwebet die Helden und singet vom Streit:

The Germanic people stride
through the primeval forest night,
Drawn forth to the fight, to the holy battle.
Oak trees arrayed in a twilight circle
Rustle so fearfully, whisper so quietly,
As if the mighty body of warriors should be
Struck by foreboding, overcome by grief.
They move forward, however, with powerful tread,
Like thunder approaches with flash of lightning!
And out from the wild, gloomy oaken boughs
A song resounds, now growing louder,
For the guardian company of Valkyries
Surround the heros and sing of the battle:

In Odin's Hallen ist es licht
und fern der Erdenpein,
aus Freyas' Wonnestrahlen
bricht die Seligkeit herein!
Solgofnin ruft den gold'nen Tag
und Bragas Harfe klingt,
mit Balmungschlag und im Gelag
die süße Zeit entschwingt.
Wer mutig für das Höchste ficht,
der geht zu Göttern ein!
O, Liebe ist's, die uns beschwingt,
zu künden das Geschick:
Der Kampf nun winkt, ihr Alle sinkt,
und keiner kehrt zurück!

Light illuminates Odin's Hall,
Far from earthly pain,
Freya's rays of rapture,
Shine forth in heavenly bliss.
Solgofnir calls forth the golden day,
And Braga's harp is heard
With Balmung's sword-clash,
And at the Feast sweet time ceases.
He who fights boldly for the highest principles
Can join the Gods!
O, it is Love that drives us
To tell of our fate.
Battle beckons, all are stricken,
And none returns.

Da schlagen die Krieger mit wilder Gewalt
die Schwerter zum Schild,
daß es hallt und erschallt!
"Und soll denn dies Schreiten
das letzte auch sein,
so wollen wir gerne dem Tode uns weih'n.

Then strike the warriors
with ferocious force,
Sword against shield,
Echoing and reverberating!
"And even if this engagement
Should also be our last,
We gladly consecrate ourselves to Death.
Nevertheless, from this bold undertaking

Doch möge aus diesem so mutigen Zieh'n
der Segen der Heimat, das Siegen erbl-
üh'n!
Teutonias Söhne, mit freundigem Mut,
sie geben so gerne ihr Leben und Blut!
Die Freiheit, die Heimat ja ewig bestehn,
die flüchtigen Güter, sie mögen ver-
gehn!"
So riefen die Krieger, so zogen sie fort,
gesegnet ihr Tun und bewahret ihr Wort!

Our homeland's blessing and victory blossom!
Teutonic sons, with joyous courage
Gladly give their life and blood!
Freedom and homeland endure forever,
Worldly things are transitory, passing away!"
Thus the warriors declared, moving forth,
Their deeds blessed, their words pre-served.

(Proffitt 1991, 9–11)

Bruckner scored the accompaniment for a brass band consisting of: two soprano cornets in E-flat and B-flat, tenorhorn, four horns, four trumpets, three trombones, and tuba. The band of the Hessen Regiment in Linz played the premiere (Göllerich/Auer 1974, III/1: 209). The instrumentation indicates that this was a Cavalry band. In the German-speaking countries, bands associated with mounted troops retained an all-brass character throughout the nineteenth-century. After the 1851 reorganization of all military music within the Austrian Empire, such bands were restricted to about twenty-four musicians (Whitwell 1984, 5: 60–64). Bruck-ner's score calls for fifteen players, but apparently a mass choir was available (Göllerich/Auer 1974, III/1: 207), so it seems likely that the entire complement of the Regiment's bandsmen were involved—probably about two dozen musicians.

Bruckner structured his work in three movements according to the versification of the text. Because the imagery of the first and third stanzas is similar, much of the music from the first movement recurs in the third. Bruckner added another structural level as well. Each movement consists of two verses that begin in identical fashion but end in significantly different ways. Another important aspect of the form is the bridging, or near-bridging, of all the movements. The first movement cadences on the dominant—A major. In the final bar all of the per-formers, except the four horns, release after two beats. The horns continue to sustain the A major chord under a *fermata*. While the horn quartet does not actually bridge the two movements, linkage is implied by the ensuing harmony. Movement two is in A major, and begins on a dominant seventh in that key. The chord sequence over the break between the movements is I → V^7 → I in A major—a common opening progression in tonal music. The movements are timbrally linked as well. The second movement is scored for solo quartet and four horns, making the final chord of the first movement seem to belong to the following music.

Movements two and three are actually bridged. The second movement is completed by a brief passage for solo horn that is closely related to motivic material earlier in the work. It is, in effect, a decoration of the pitch A, which is the tonic of movement two and the dominant of movement three. Its dotted rhythm leads directly into the next movement.

Example 4.12:
Germanenzug, Mvt. 2, bar 38–39, Mvt. 3, bar 1

Bruckner's linking of the movements of this work was probably inspired by the poem, which presents a single, unified plot line. Such considerations had become part of his thinking. As indicated earlier in this chapter, when he was faced with a similar problem between the second and third movements of the *Festcantata: Preiset den Herrn*, he found a comparable solution. However, a stronger impetus to develop this concept may have come from his study of Wagner's *Tannhäuser*. Numerous examples of the bridging and near-bridging of scenes can be found throughout this score, illustrating Wagner's principle of continuous thematic development—both musically and dramatically.

Movement one consists of a ten-bar instrumental introduction and two verses. The verses are altered only during their concluding five bars, and, while the style is similar, they cadence in different keys—D major and A major, respectively. The introduction is dramatic and presents a number of musical ideas that are central to the construction of the piece.

Example 4.13:
Germanenzug, Mvt. I, bars 1–6

The first sounds of the work are three octaves of a unison D, set melodically as several descending octave skips in dotted rhythm. After three bars the motivic profile is smoothed but the dotted rhythm persists. Only the initial bar is in unison. In the ensuing measures a powerful series of third-related chords appears and leads to a cadence on the dominant with a familiar progression—German sixth → tonic.

All of the above are hallmarks of Bruckner's mature style and clearly identify this piece with him. They are also very important compositional germs of this entire work. Dotted rhythms characterize all movements, and melodies featuring descending octaves occur frequently. Unison-to-harmony textures appear in virtually every phrase of the outer movements, but are found less frequently in the solo quartet. Much of the harmony and the key structure is third-related.

The rest of the introduction also displays unmistakable Brucknerian traits, and presents significant source material. At bar six the texture is abruptly reduced to a single line and in the next bar a solo cornet introduces an important melodic motive consisting of an upper neighbour/lower neighbour decoration of the dominant of the new key. Similar motives can be found in the main themes of many Bruckner symphonies (Göllerich/Auer 1974, III/1: 207). In this case it is employed symphonically. Many derivatives of this idea appear in all movements of *Germanenzug*, including the horn passage that bridges movement two and three (see Example 4.12).

Example 4.14:
Germanenzug, **Mvt. I, bars 7, 11, 13, 17**

When the choir enters at bar eleven, the unison-to-harmony texture[22] of the initial bars recurs and is repeated. In fact, most of the words that directly mention warriors and battles are set in unison, perhaps a reference to the ancient tradition of singing battle and marching songs in unison. Most of the verse is sparingly accompanied by the low register instruments, which usually simplify the choral lines but sometimes contribute additional harmony and highlight important motives from the choral textures. The choral writing is contrapuntal, but with the exception of one brief passage at the words "Oak trees ... circle," is not imitative. The accompanimental texture is thickened at the conclusion of the verse to create a climax.

The first verse contains one stunning example of tone painting and one passage of familiar harmonic writing. Bruckner set the words "whisper so quietly"[23] in unison and with a *decrescendo*. Then "so quietly" is repeated in harmony at a

---

[22]This textural idea is reinforced by the dynamics. Each unison phrase is marked *piano* with a *crescendo* leading into the harmonized segments.

[23]Melodically, this passage is another variation of the solo cornet motive from the introduction.

pianissimo dynamic. The next phrase presents a stream of sixth chords over a dominant pedal.

Example 4.15:
Germanenzug, Mvt. I, bars 17–21 (voices only)

Verse two is essentially identical to verse one. The words "They move forward, however ... lightening" necessitated some expansion of the accompaniment and much more dramatic *crescendi* through the initial unison-to-harmony phrases. The ending is forceful, and the B♭M → Dm → AM progression echoes the opening bars.

Movement two is the "Song of the Valkyries," the mounted maidens of Norse mythology who collected fallen heros and transported them to paradise in Valhalla (Hamilton 1963, 309). In Silberstein's poem they describe the glory of Valhalla in order to urge the Teutonic warriors on to battle.[24] Set as an *adagio* for quartets of singers and horns, the music of the Valkyries' song is made expressive through on-the-beat dissonance, frequent suspensions, and delayed resolutions of seventh chords that make many bars difficult to analyze harmonically. Like the previous movement it consists of two stanzas; however, the verses are identical in this instance. Contrast is provided by a brief coda and a curious intermediary section between the verses that functions as a *cadenza* for the singers.

This movement is ostensibly in A major, but the key is barely established when the music turns toward the sub-mediant. The words "*ist es licht*" are set to three third-related chords (AM → F♯m → C♯M) that Bruckner said were intended to represent the brightness of Odin's hall. "See, now it becomes bright," he is reported to have explained to the performers during rehearsals for the premiere (Göllerich/-Auer 1974, III/1: 208). The next phrase is also striking. The words are "Far from earthly pain," and the music is in unison and is whispered by the male quartet. A horn echo,[25] perhaps signal from distant Valhalla, concludes these original and engaging phrases.

---

[24]Bruckner was especially fond of this part of *Germanenzug*, and, as discussed earlier, requested that it be performed at his funeral. Presumably, he saw himself as a hero fallen in an epic and holy battle.

[25]Musically, this motive is derived from the solo cornet motive that initially appeared in bar seven of the first movement.

Example 4.16:
Germanenzug, Mvt. 2, bars 2–4

The final bars of this verse contain another remarkable example of tone painting. At the words "Solgofnir calls forth the golden day," a horn solo appears that
is reminiscent of the opening motive of the work, and at the same time the two bass
voices *arpeggiate* a G major chord, also in the style of a horn call. These figures
are no doubt intended to represent the cries of Solgofnir, the golden cockerel, as
he rouses the Gods at dawn.

Example 4.17:
Germanenzug, Mvt. 2, bars 12–14

Hawkshaw quotes two letters written by Bruckner to Rudolf Weinwurm in late
February and early March 1864 while he was preparing *Germanenzug* for publication. In these letters he discusses the possibility of adding a harp part to the
score (Hawkshaw 1990, 22). At first glance harp would seem an odd addition to
a score that uses only brass instruments, but the incongruity is explained when one
considers the next phrase of text—"And Braga's harp is heard." Braga was Norse
God of poetry (Hamilton 1963, 325), and was often portrayed playing harp. A
silent *fermata* indicates the end of verse one.[26]

Between the verses, an unusual interlude appears that was identified earlier as
a *cadenza* for the voices. In a florid style unlike anything else in this work, each
singer in turn assumes the lead, enunciating the words "With Balmung's sword
clash ... sweet time ceases." The slow harmonic rhythm and improvisatory nature

---

[26]*Fermatas* are a significant element of Bruckner's mature style, and were often ridiculed.
He explained them by saying, "Whenever I have something new and important to say, I must
stop and take a breath first." (Watson 1977, 73). In this movement pauses appear at the end
of each verse, and do indeed usher in "something new and important"—the voice *cadenza*
after the first verse, and the coda, with its surprising *phrygian* scale, after the second.

of these bars does indeed give the impression that, both harmonically and melodically, the forward momentum of the music has ceased.[27]

The second verse exactly duplicates the first. In fact, Bruckner repeated the first two lines of the Valkyrie song, text and music, at the beginning of verse two. Some of this music seems considerably less integrated with the words. For example, the passage that depicted Solgofnir's wake-up calls so effectively in verse one is attached to "O, it is love that drives us" in this verse. The fanfare-like style of this passage is difficult to reconcile with the textual phrase. While the music remains attractive, the imagery it originally portrayed has disappeared.

This movement ends with a short coda. The words are the final couplet of the stanza, and Bruckner has again projected the battle image with unison writing. The full ensemble (voices and horns) join in a melodic fragment based on an E-*phrygian* scale that ultimately breaks into harmony at the cadence. The cadence itself is unconventional. The chords are all related by thirds, and, while the final sonority is the tonic of the movement (A major), the preceding chords seem to be drawn from the parallel minor.[28]

Example 4.18:
Germanenzug, Mvt. 2, bars 36–38

The final movement begins with a reprise of the introduction and the first verse of movement one. A slight change occurs at the second choral phrase, which employs a much bigger *crescendo* and a fuller accompaniment than in the initial movement, undoubtedly because the words "Sword against shield, echoing and reverberating!" present a much more active image. The battle is no longer being contemplated; the enemy has been engaged. The carefully constructed echo at the words "whisper so quietly" in the first movement (see Example 4.15) seems less

---

[27]It is not difficult to imagine that, if these bars been written a century later, they would have been notated *senza misura*.

[28]This structure approximates a *phrygian* cadence. Its appearance here, at the beginning of a bridging passage to the next movement, reflects the traditional use of this cadence in tonal music—as a transition from one movement to another (Apel 1972, 669).

appropriate to the new words, "Consecrate ourselves to death," but does work on an intellectual, abstract level.

After the reprise the remainder of this movement is new material. This part of the work consists of large climaxes and *a capella* passages that are timbrally and stylistically reminiscent of the second-movement quartet but are not exact restatements. The first climax, at the words "Freedom and Homeland endure forever," is built from the horn fanfare that opened the *Cantata: Auf, Brüder! auf... Hand!* of 1855 (see Example 2.15), but in this instance it is scored forcefully for the full ensemble. An *a capella* passage at the words "Worldly things are transitory, passing away," displays some impressive contrary-motion counterpoint between first tenor and first bass, while the other two voices provide a dominant pedal.

Example 4.19:
Germanenzug, Mvt. 3, bars 33–35

Like many Brucknerian endings, the concluding statement begins as a towering unison that opens into harmony. The music passes quickly through E-flat major and D minor before cadencing in D major.

This music, energetic and somewhat primitive, catches the sense of the primeval and the timelessness projected by the myth: "Its florid passion in evoking pagan Valhalla [the second movement] verges on the unique within the composer's canon, coming as close to operatic writing as he ever did" (Proffitt 1991, 4).

Bruckner's musical imagination, his often pictorial reflection of the text, and his attention to detail produced a major contribution to the repertoire for winds and chorus. Unlike all works previously reviewed in this study, *Germanenzug* is completely in Bruckner's new style with hardly a backward glance toward earlier music. Harmonic usage is fully nineteenth-century, centred around root progressions and key contrasts in thirds. Particularly in the second movement, substantial passages appear where no more than a few chords can be analyzed in any one key. The instruments are more independent of the voices than in previous works in this genre by Bruckner. While they continue to double and to support the choir, they also add extra harmony and contrapuntal lines, and contribute substantially to the effectiveness of the tone painting. The year that had passed between the composition of the *Festcantata: Preiset den Herrn* and this work had had a monumental impact on this composer's thinking. With new development in his ability to realize his harmonic, formal and timbral ideas, Bruckner was indeed a professional composer, well on his way to a unique place in the musical literature.

MARSCH IN ES-DUR—WAB 116

Very little is known about the genesis of this work. The autograph manuscript is dated "Linz, August 12, 1865," and the march is dedicated to the military band of *Jäger-Truppe* (Rifleman's Company) in Linz[29] (Grasberger 1977, 129). Göllerich and Auer speculate that since Bruckner had established contact with the military bands in Linz through the composition and performance of the *Festcantata: Preiset den Herrn* and *Germanenzug*, this connection led to the commissioning of the march (Göllerich/Auer 1974, III/1: 322). However, no specific evidence supporting this contention or documentation confirming a first performance has been found (Bornhöft 1996, preface).

It seems overstated to assert that Bruckner's connections with Linz military bands inspired the composition of the *March in E-flat Major*. The scoring of the *Festcantata* was orchestral in concept and does not match any of the standard military band instrumentations of the time. Also, since Bruckner did not conduct the premiere, his contacts with local bands would have been tangential at best. *Germanenzug* presents a better case, since it appears to have been scored for a specific Linz Cavalry band. However, the instrumentation of the *March in E-flat* indicates that it was intended for an *infantry* band.[30] It is not clear how Bruckner's association with a Cavalry band might have resulted in the composition of a march for a radically different instrumentation.

In the Bruckner literature the *March in E-flat* is always associated with the *Apollo-Marsch*, a work that has now been proven to have been written in 1857 by Kéler Béla (Probst 1984, 6). Unquestionably, the two marches display a number of similarities. Both are in E-flat major with a trio in the subdominant, both employ a similar form, and both use an identical instrumentation (Hawkshaw 1989, 10). It is generally accepted that Bruckner used the *Apollo-Marsch* as a model when composing his own march, but it's difficult to ascertain when he may have acquired the score. He studied the march form with Kitzler in January 1862 (Hawkshaw 1984, 86, 95), and may have been given this piece as an example of the structure at that time. On the other hand, the score may have been provided by the conductor of the Linz *Jäger* band when Bruckner was composing the *March in E♭ Major* during the summer of 1865.

Bruckner's *E♭ Major March* is cast in one of the traditional march forms—two

---

[29]The Austrian National Library holds both the holograph manuscript (call number Mus. Hs. 3168) and a fair copy (call number Mus. Hs. 6027) in the hand of Franz Schimatschek, Bruckner's principal Linz copyist (Hawkshaw 1989, 10). The library has graciously provided the author with copies of both manuscripts.

[30]The March is scored for D-flat flute (probably implies piccolo as well), A-flat clarinet, two E-flat clarinets, three B-flat clarinets, four horns, two B-flat flügelhorns, five E-flat trumpets, two B-flat trumpets, three euphoniums, two trombones, two basses, and percussion. This instrumentation does not differ substantially from that of the typical Austrian infantry band of the time (Whitwell 1984, 5: 63).

strains, both repeated, a trio with two repeated sections, and a *da capo*. Both the march and the trio are in rounded binary form, which adds an unusual degree of structural precision. Also, in accordance with the accepted norms of the genre, the second strain is in the dominant and the trio in the subdominant. However, beyond these basic principles, the march is anything but harmonically conventional. Especially during the first strain, Bruckner consistently places long, non-chord tones on strong beats, which, when combined with chromatic voice leading, enliven the underlying straightforward chord sequences to create a vivid harmonic context.

Example 4.20:
March in E-flat—bars 5–8

Bruckner's melodic usage is also unconventional for this genre. The primary motive is sometimes developed canonically, and the melody-carriers frequently leap into sharp dissonance—a procedure that must have surprised the military musicians of the day—providing, that is, they ever played this march at all.

Example 4.21:
March in E-flat—bars 28–29

The second strain, scored initially for brass alone, is simpler harmonically. All of the new material is over a B-flat pedal, and the harmonic rhythm is much slower. At the second phrase, the key jumps abruptly from B-flat major to G-flat major, reflecting Bruckner's fondness for tonalities that descend by major thirds. The key descends by another third, to E-flat major, for the reprise of the first bars of the march.

The trio features beautiful two-part counterpoint, initially between E-flat trumpets and flügelhorns, later between E-flat trumpets/flügelhorns and euphoniums.

Example 4.22:
March in E-flat—bars 33–36 (counterpoint only)

Like the second strain, this part of the march has a slow harmonic rhythm grounded on pedals, but several extraordinary progressions appear.

Example 4.23:
March in E-flat—bars 41–45 (harmony only)

During the summer of 1865, when this work was composed, Bruckner's main energies were directed to the creation of his *Symphony No. 1 in C minor*. The melodic material of the march, much of it marked by sixth skips within *arpeggiated* figures, is reminiscent of the thematic content of the Symphony, but only one brief motive is directly quoted. In the second strain, as Bruckner was preparing the return of the principal theme, a descending octave figure appears in the high woodwinds. This motive occurs repeatedly throughout the first movement of *Symphony No. 1*, always in the winds, and functioning exactly as it does in the march—preparing major climactic points.[31]

Example 4.24A:
March in E-flat—bars 21–24

Example 4.24B:
Symphony No. 1, Mvt. 1, bars 261–63

---

[31]The quotation from *Symphony No. 1* that appears below is drawn from the Critical Edition of the "Linz version" of this work, prepared by Robert Haas, and published in 1935.

The reaction of nineteenth-century military bandsmen to this music appears to be reflected in the fact that no performance during Bruckner's lifetime is recorded (Göllerich/Auer 1974, III/1: 648–49). Perhaps military conductors felt that this music's harmonic complexity and delicate scoring would prevent it from sounding well in outdoor performance venues. In fact, their concerns may have been justified. Without careful attention to balance and the precise resolution of dissonance, the numerous non harmonic tones in the melody could give the impression that the high voices and the low voices were playing in different keys.

If the *Apollo-Marsch* was indeed Bruckner's model, he outstripped it in virtually every musical parameter. The *Apollo-Marsch* is a pleasant, tuneful work that by-and-large uses only the common chords within the key, and rarely deploys less than the full ensemble. Bruckner's fascination with instrumental colour and his harmonic originality did not permit him to compose a similar piece, even when his purpose was to create a straightforward, functional work. His inventiveness probably removed the *March in E-flat* from the purview of nineteenth-century military bands, but in concert performance, where balance and rhythmic precision can be controlled, the work sounds fresh and varied, and is clearly an important addition to this repertoire.

INVENI DAVID—WAB 19

In January, 1868, Bruckner was reappointed conductor of the *Liedertafel* "*Frohsinn*"[32] (Watson 1977, 23). A few months later, in April and May 1868, the choir commemorated the anniversary of its founding with a series of special concerts, one of which was a concert performance of the Finale to Act III of *Die Meistersinger*[33] (Schönzeler 1970, 48). Bruckner's offertory, *Inveni David*, was written for the anniversary festival, and is dedicated to the choir[34] (Grasberger 1977, 23).

---

[32]Bruckner had previously served as the conductor of this fine choir from November 1860 (Watson 1977, 17), until September 1861. He resigned over an incident that took place in Nürnburg, which the choir was visiting for a choral festival. As a joke, the singers sent a seductively dressed waitress to his room. Bruckner saw this incident as an insult, not a joke, and promptly resigned his conductorship (Schönzeler 1970, 42).

[33]Wagner himself had suggested that Bruckner perform this music. The performance, on April 4, 1868, was the first public presentation of any part of *Die Meistersinger* (Schönzeler 1970, 48).

[34]The dedication reads: "Respectfully dedicated to the laudable choral society on the occasion of the celebration of foundation. Offertorium for men's choir accompanied by 4 trombones, April 21, 1868. Anton Bruckner, choirmaster" ["der löblichen Liedertafel achtungsvollst gewidmet zum Gründungsfest. Offertorium für Männerchor in Begleitung von 4 Trombonen, 21. April 1868. Anton Bruckner, Chormeister"] (Göllerich/Auer 1974, III/1: 441).

The words are drawn from Psalm 88 (verses 20-21) in the Vulgate numbering system, but, more importantly, are the text of the offertory of the first Common Mass for a Confessor Bishop (*Liber Usualis* 1952, 385, 1185):

Inveni David servum meum,	I have selected my servant David,
Oleo sancto meo unxi eum,	And anointed him with my sacred oil,
Manus enim mea auxiliabitur ei	My hand will be constantly with him,
Et brachium meum confortabit eum.	And my arm will strengthen him.
Alleluja	Alleluia

(Proffitt 1991, 11)

Bruckner completed the work on April 21, 1868 (Grasberger 1977, 23). Since it was written immediately following the historic performance of the excerpt from *Die Meistersinger*, some writers have suggested it was intended to show the composer's appreciation to his choir for its fine performance of a work that meant a great deal to him (Proffitt 1991, 5). It seems likely that the date of its first performance was more significant. *Inveni David* was premiered on May 10, 1868, by the *Liedertafel "Frohsinn"* under Bruckner's baton (Grasberger 1977, 23). The feast of St. Antoninus, Bishop and Confessor, is celebrated on May 10, and the first Common Mass for Confessor Bishops is specified for that observance (*Liber Usualis* 1952, 1465). It would appear that, knowing the date on which the work would be performed, the composer drew on his broad knowledge of the Catholic liturgy to select a text appropriate for that day.[35]

The scoring of this work, male chorus and four trombones, is unique in Bruckner's output. Except for a lost *Requiem* from 1845, no other liturgical composition employs male chorus. The use of four trombones recalls an earlier work, *Laßt Jubeltöne laut erklingen*, and in both pieces the trombones function in essentially the same way; that is, they double the four voice parts. However, in *Laßt Jubeltöne* the trombones are only part of the accompanying forces. That work requires a full brass ensemble, including trumpets and horns.

The opening phrase establishes a number of harmonic principles that will be explored throughout the piece. Unison voices outline the tonic triad, F minor, and place the sub-mediant (D♭) in a prominent rhythmic position—on the downbeat of the second bar. This placement is significant for the first cadence (bar 4), which is on a D-flat major chord. The first chord to appear (bar 3) is the Neapolitan, G-flat major.[36] It persists for six beats before resolving to the aforementioned D-flat in a

---

[35]The work, however, makes no apparent reference to the plainchant associated with this text, unless the numerous upper-neighbour figures in the chant are seen as the inspiration for the frequent Neapolitan chords in Bruckner's setting.

[36]Bruckner showed a decided fondness for Neapolitan relationships in many of his later compositions. These are especially notable in the *Symphony No. 6* and the *String Quintet in*

(continued...)

plagal cadence. All of these harmonic issues are important to the construction of the piece. Neapolitan chords appear frequently, sometimes in surprising contexts, and half-step root movement, especially between phrases, defines much of the chord selection. A significant number of the cadences throughout the work are plagal.

Example 4.25:
Inveni David—bars 1–4

At the second phrase both the half-step progression and the Neapolitan relationship are immediately apparent. After the D-flat chord that concluded the first phrase, the bass moves down a half-step to C, and initiates a series of entries of a motive that leaps up an octave. Voices two and three enter together in parallel thirds, with the third voice a semi-tone above the bass. These two voices create a D-flat major chord (over a C suspended from the preceding bar), putting them into a Neapolitan relationship with the previous bar.

Example 4.26:
Inveni David—bars 5–8

The tonality of the rest of this phrase is unclear, but it ultimately cadences in C major, the dominant of the initial key. The trombones double the voices through much of this phrase, undoubtedly to assist the singers in negotiating the complex chordal structure that often has voices entering or leaping into sharp dissonance.

The words "*unxi eum*" end the second phrase and begin the third. During the repeat of this textual fragment, the tonality established at the end of phrase two, C major, dissolves through another Neapolitan chord (with an articulated, suspended

---

[36](...continued)
F, but can be found in nearly all of his mature compositions (Watson 1977, 77).

C in the bass) to G-flat major. It touches on the dominant and the mediant of the
new key, then settles on a C-flat major chord for five full bars—the longest period
of harmonic stability in the entire composition. C-flat major, the lowered dominant
of the original key, is as remote from the tonic, F minor, as is possible within the
confines of tonal music, but in this instance it may be further development of a
harmonic principle that is central to the conception of this piece. The progression
that prepares the arrival of the C-flat major chord, G♭M → D♭M → B♭M →
C♭M, means that the C-flat chord is in Neapolitan relationship to the chord that
precedes it.

Example 4.27:
Inveni David—bars 14–17

This long passage of C-flat major sonority is coloured at its fourth bar by a
semi-tone ascent in the first bass. This movement creates a brief augmented chord
that is aurally intriguing and seems to have been borrowed from Wagner.[37] It also
draws attention to the fourth syllable of the word "*auxiliabitur*" (will be constantly
with [him]).[38]

Example 4.28:
Inveni David—bars 18–19

Chromatic voice leading permits Bruckner to transform the C-flat major chord
into a dominant seventh on G, which leads to another cadence in C major, and to

---

[37]Bruckner had, of course, been heavily involved with the preparation of the final scene
from *Die Meistersinger* immediately prior to composing this work.

[38]An identical ascent in the first bass recurs two bars later on the same word, but in a
different harmonic context. At this point the C-flat major chord is transformed into a
dominant seventh on G—a surprising progression, but considerably less astringent than the
augmented chord two bars earlier.

the return of the first bars of the piece. The choir restates the unison opening phrase exactly as it initially appeared, but is accompanied by the trombones, which make explicit the implied harmony. A transition built around the dominant chord © Major) leads to a dramatic modulation to F major, the key of the extensive coda.

The only text enunciated throughout the coda is the one word, "*Alleluja*," and the music is exuberant and resonant. Although no tempo change is specified, the music seems more animated because of the responsive texture, the predominance of major chords, and the voicing, which often places wide intervals between the two lowest voices. Essentially, the music consists of a series of cadences, some authentic, some plagal. The final cadence, I → V → I over a tonic pedal, is reminiscent of *Afferentur regi*.[39]

Until the coda the trombones are used rather sparingly. For the most part their function is to guide the pitch of the choir through the unorthodox harmonic sequences, mostly by providing a few chords at critical junctures. Occasionally, they sound through otherwise silent bars. During the coda they are much more active and contribute substantially to the dramatic character of this music.

Inveni David is among the few wind-chorus works by Bruckner that have achieved lasting popularity, and appear regularly on concert programs. Such attention to this composition is not surprising, considering its well-integrated compositional technique, intriguing harmony, and effective use of the performing forces. This music attracts the listener's ear, and, at the same time, seems to flow completely naturally from chord to chord and from phrase to phrase. When compared to other liturgical works previously reviewed in this study, *Inveni David* employs similar techniques—unison passages opening into harmony, responsive and imitative textures contrasted with block harmonies, and so on—but their effect is completely different in this context. In earlier compositions these techniques looked backwards, establishing Bruckner's connections to the rich traditions of religious music. In this work these procedures anticipate future developments and stretch the boundaries not only of sacred music, but of tonal music itself. By 1868 Bruckner was a fully "modern" composer who, consciously or unconsciously, was remaking every genre he chose to take up.

---

[39]Göllerich and Auer suggest that this *Alleluia*, and especially its cadence, was influenced by Händel's famous *Halleluia*, which Bruckner often used in his improvisations (Göllerich/-Auer 1974, III/1: 443). Both the rhythm and the responsive texture support this view.

Chapter 5

` The *E-Minor Mass—WAB 27*

This magnificent composition is Bruckner's most significant contribution to the wind-chorus literature, and is one of the monuments of the choral repertoire generally. Its creation was initiated by Bishop Franz Josef Rudigier of Linz, and like the *Festcantata: Preiset den Herrn*, it was associated with the Bishop's major enterprise for his diocese—the construction of a new cathedral. Rudigier is believed to have commissioned the Mass on May 1, 1862, the day when Bruckner's *Festcantata: Preiset den Herrn* was premiered at the ceremonies marking the laying of the cornerstone for the new cathedral. The new Mass was intended for performance at the consecration of the Votive Chapel, which was to be constructed at the apex of the apse of the cathedral (Nowak 1977, iii). Bruckner did not begin composition for several years. He finished the work on November 25, 1866[1] (Grasberger 1977, 31), but construction delays postponed the completion of the Chapel, and the *Mass in E Minor* was not premiered until Michaelmas Day, September 29, 1869. By this time Bruckner had been resident in Vienna for more than a year. He returned to Linz to participate in the festivities by conducting his Mass,[2] and later commented that this was "one of the greatest days of my life ...The Bishop and the representative of the Emperor drank a toast to me at the episcopal banquet" (Nowak 1977, iii–iv).

Bruckner revised the score during the summer of 1876, and substantially

---

[1]Bruckner announced the completion of the work in a letter to Weinwurm dated December 2, 1866: "The Mass for eight-voice chorus with wind instrument accompaniment, for the consecration of the Votive Chapel is completed" (Göllerich/Auer 1974, III/1: 365).

[2]The choir at the first performance included members of the *Liedertafel "Frohsinn,"* the *Sängerbund*, and the *Musikverein*. The accompaniment was performed by representatives from the band of the Austro-Hungarian infantry regiment, *Ernst Ludwig, Großherzog von Hessen und bei Rhein Nr. 14* (Nowak 1977, iii).

rewrote it in 1882. Leopold Nowak has studied these emendations in considerable detail and reports that their chronology cannot be precisely determined. In his 1977 edition of the original (1866) score, published in the *Collected Works*, Nowak included a chart that details the differences between the two versions. The final version, which Nowak considers representative of Bruckner's ultimate thoughts on this music,[3] was premiered in the Old Cathedral in Linz on October 4, 1885, at the conclusion of the celebrations marking the centennial of the diocese. Bruckner did not conduct, but apparently "stood near the organ with his eyes uplifted ecstatically to the vaulted roof, his lips moving in silent prayer" (Nowak 1959, iii–iv).

The work was scored for eight-part mixed chorus and fifteen wind players —two oboes, two clarinets, two bassoons, four horns, two trumpets, and three trombones. It has long been believed that the wind scoring was dictated by the circumstances of the first performance—in the open air outside the new cathedral in Linz (Nowak 1977, iii). However, an 1869 letter from Bruckner to Schieder-mayer, the dean of the cathedral, contains an interesting implication: "Unfortunately there is not sufficient space in the choir, but, after all, we can always perform it in the open (Schönzeler 1970, 144).

This letter suggests that the work was originally intended for presentation inside the Chapel, and that the wind scoring was an essential part of the initial conception of the piece. Ernst Kurth believes this to have been the case:

The immediate reason for the wind scoring might have been the consideration of a performance at the cathedral of Linz, but the exclusion of the string instruments also refers to an adaption of the style to that of a time when music was not yet filled with their more sensitive creation of sound. There is something of chastity, something that gets closer to the character of the old church, and at the same time something rural in the use of wind instruments. (Kurth 1971, II: 1217)

Although no evidence exists confirming Bruckner's view, other composers felt that the "espressivo" character of string instruments was inappropriate for some music based on archaic antecedents.[4] The outdoor performance, then, appears not to have influenced the original instrumentation, but was something of a circumstantial "accident" that arose when the Chapel proved to be too small to accommodate

---

[3]Some conductors disagree. Margaret Hillis (the conductor of the Chicago Symphony Chorus), for example, prefers the original (1866) version (Hillis 1991, 90). Clearly both versions are authentic, and both are certainly worthy of performance.

[4]Stravinsky, for example, featured wind instruments in many of his early Neoclassical compositions. About his *Octuor* he said:

"Wind instruments seem to me to be more apt to render a certain rigidity of the form....The suppleness of the string instruments can lend itself to more subtle nuances and can serve better the individual sensibility of the executant in works built on an 'emotive' basis" (White 1984, 574–75).

the performers. In this Mass Bruckner was attempting to create a work that would stand apart from much of the sacred music being written at the time. The wind inst-rument accompaniment may well have been an important part of the process of distancing it from its Romantic relatives.

Bruckner's use of the instruments is both economical and imaginative. Much of the time they assist the singers through complex harmonic sequences by doub-ling or simplifying choral parts. At other times; however, they present their own lines, which energize the rhythm, highlight important words or musical phrases, or contribute to the poetic realization of the text. While generally restricted to a supporting role, they are essential to the constantly evolving soundscape of the work, and add immeasurably to its unity and power.[5]

The archaic style of this composition has elicited much comment, especially since the two large sacred works that frame it chronologically, the Masses in D minor and F minor, are so flamboyantly Romantic.[6] Of the three great masses, the *Mass in E Minor* is the most obviously liturgical in concept.[7] Grounded in traditional styles, it recalls many of the age-old ritual practices of the Roman Catholic church, including intoned plainsong, hints of *versicle-response*, and *antiphony*. The first phrases of both the *Gloria* and the *Credo* are missing from Bruckner's setting, an acknowledgment that in the liturgy these phrases are sung by the celebrant alone. Compositionally, this work draws on the contrapuntal pro-cedures of the sixteenth century, especially those of Palestrina, who is recalled directly in the *Sanctus*.

There seems to be little doubt that the conception of the *E-minor Mass* was influenced by the Cecilian movement. Bruckner, like many other sacred-music composers of the time, was initially attracted by the idealism of the Cecilians, and counted Ignaz Traumihler, choir master at St. Florian and an arch-Cecilianist,

---

[5]Bruckner researchers make reference to an alternative version of this work scored for vo-ices accompanied by organ alone. While Bruckner may have contemplated such a version or at least considered adding organ to the score, none of the manuscripts contain a part for this instrument (Redlich 1955, 74).

An arrangement in which the organ replaced the wind instruments was prepared by Vincenz Goller, and was published in Vienna by Universal Edition. This arrangement rec-eived the enthusiastic endorsement of Kurth and Göllerich and Auer (see Kurth 1971, II: 1217; Göllerich/Auer 1974, III/1: 372), but, since Bruckner resisted adding organ despite revising the score several times, it seems that he heard this work only in its original instru-mentation.

[6]One is reminded of Liszt's comment, "The Church composer is both preacher and priest" (La Mara 1968, I: 315–16). In Bruckner's *oeuvre* one might suggest that while the Masses in D minor and F minor represent the "preacher" in church music, the *E-minor Mass* assumes the role of "priest."

[7]Ernst Kurth describes it as "tender and ascetic, like a great hymn to Mary" (Kurth 1971, II: 1216).

among his friends [8] (Redlich 1955, 72). A small group of his religious works were written to conform to Cecilian principles, including parts (especially the *Sanctus*) of this Mass.[9] Bruckner undoubtedly was pleased that his Mass was well received by the Cecilians, but ultimately he, like most innovative composers, found their dogmatism too restrictive and turned away from the movement. He was also infuriated when, in 1885, Witt published the *Pange lingua*, but "corrected" some of its most poignant dissonances (Watson 1977, 99). Although the *Mass in E Minor* takes its inspiration from the vocal polyphony of the high Renaissance, especially that of Palestrina, the harmony, the instrumental writing, and the chromatic development of motives reflect Bruckner's musical thinking at its most inventive. This is a work of astonishing originality that seems to, simultaneously, look far back into the past and well into the future.

KYRIE

Kyrie eleison.   Lord have mercy.
Christe eleison.   Christ have mercy.
Kyrie eleison.   Lord have mercy.

Like the text, the music of the *Kyrie* is tripartite in structure. Bruckner brings an unusual degree of individualism and musical unity to the form by recalling textures and by employing related motives from section to section; however, texture provides most of the contrast as well. This movement is virtually unaccompanied since the instruments (horns and trombones) contribute only a few chords and are marked optional.

The influence of sixteenth-century style is apparent from the outset. An archaic-sounding perfect fifth appears between the first two voice entries, the initial phrase is in *E-phrygian*, and this music is conceived linearly. The voices move

---

[8]This movement was initiated by K. Proske in the middle of the nineteenth-century. Its aim was the revision of music in the Roman Catholic church by returning to the purity of modal, unaccompanied, contrapuntal composition in the style of Palestrina. All instruments were to be banned, and all "theatrical" aspects, such as chromatic harmony, were to be avoided. Its primary exponent was Franz Xaver Witt, who founded the *Allgemeiner Deutscher Caecilienverein* in 1869 (Apel 1972, 139).

[9]The other works were the *Jam lucis* and *Pange lingua*, both written in 1868, and both in *phrygian* mode, and the *lydian* Gradual, *Os justi*, which was composed in 1879 and was dedicated to Traumihler (Watson 1977, 99). Bruckner has left irrefutable evidence that this latter work was conceived according to the principles of the Cecilians. On July 25, 1879, he wrote to Traumihler: "I should be very pleased if you found pleasure in the piece. It is composed without sharps and flats, without the chord of the seventh, without a six-four chord and without chordal combinations of four and five simultaneous notes" (Redlich 1955, 72).

freely over a tonic pedal, creating frequent sharp dissonance and rendering harmonic analysis superfluous. The voices enter in succession, but this music, while contrapuntal, is not imitative.[10]

Example 5.1:
E-minor Mass—Kyrie—bars 1–6

Beginning with the second phrase, the harmonic context becomes more tonal and quickly establishes a favourite Bruckner texture—parallel sixth chords over a pedal. This sub-section ultimately leads to a rather conventional cadence on the dominant (B major). To this point in the piece, only the female voices have been employed. A brief silence separates this sub-section from the next, which is scored for male voices and begins with an exact repeat of the initial phrase of the movement. This type of *antiphony* is another reflection of sixteenth-century procedures, especially those of the Venetian school (Göllerich/Auer 1974, III/1: 374). The last few bars of the initial *Kyrie* have substantial structural implications. A two-voice canon appears, which employs a subject that is closely related to several motives appearing earlier in the work, and the imitative texture anticipates the upcoming *Christe*. In addition, this exact subject, or derivatives of it, will reappear as the basis of imitative passages later in this movement and throughout the work as a whole.

Example 5.2:
E-minor Mass—Kyrie—bars 35–39

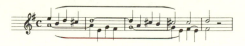

The initial *Kyrie* elides into the *Christe*, which contrasts with it by immediately developing complex imitative textures. Bruckner maintains timbral interest by beginning the *Christe* with female voices. They establish a double canon in which one of the subjects is related to the canon that appeared at the end of the initial *Kyrie* (see Example 5.2).

---

[10]Bar numbers given in all examples in this chapter are for the 1882 edition. In a number of cases they will be identical to the 1866 version, but many will vary by at least a few bars. Occasionally, especially in the *Credo*, the difference may be as much as ten bars.

Example 5.3:
*E-minor Mass—Kyrie—*bars 39–41 (subjects)

    As this section progresses the male voices are gradually added to the polyphonic texture, the choir is expanded to eight voices, and the double canon becomes a triple canon. The end of the *Christe* is one of the high points of the movement. As these climactic measures are approached, texture and harmony are simplified and the trombones add support to these loud chords.

    The second *Kyrie* is preceded by a brief silence (marked by a *fermata* in the 1882 edition). The music recalls the opening of the movement, but becomes more contrapuntal very quickly, leading to an extensive canonic development of the subject in Example 5.2—drawn from the end of the initial *Kyrie*. However, another motive is simultaneously developed in canon, and the complex imitative texture serves to recall the *Christe* as well. Also like the *Christe*, the polyphonic texture is gradually simplified as the music approaches its climax. The high point itself is very dramatic. The full ensemble participates in block-chord harmonies that function largely diatonically, but explore both E major and E minor. Following the climax the music begins a long *diminuendo* leading to a very quiet ending in E major. However, during these closing bars Bruckner added another brilliant touch of musical unity. At measure 104 the music cadences on an open fifth that signals the reintroduction of the two-voice canon that appeared at the end of the first *Kyrie*. In this case the canon is blended into simple supporting harmony that adds to the subtlety of the effect. Recalling the end of the first *Kyrie* at the close of the second provides the movement as a whole with a wonderful sense of formal balance that is rarely heard in the music of lesser composers.

    Bruckner's *Kyrie* is a marvel of musical integration and subtle contrast. Throughout the movement the similarity of motives from section to section allows the music to flow smoothly across structural divisions, but, since these motives are not identical, they generate a sense of evolution as well. Texture provides most of the contrast. Strict application of imitative devices sets the *Christe* apart from the initial *Kyrie*, but when the second *Kyrie* arrives, Bruckner uses texture to adapt the form to his musical needs. Canonic rendering of material from the initial *Kyrie* makes this section into a recapitulation of both previous sections rather than the simple repetition of initial ideas that is normally demanded by the parameters of ternary form.

    The two versions of this movement display only minor differences. In the 1882 version Bruckner adjusted some of the text alignment and extended the final cadence by two bars to provide better balance. The only other revision has significance for performance—the meter signature is altered from *alla breve* to common time. This change was important to Bruckner, and apparently was intended to ensure that this movement would be taken at a slow tempo.

GLORIA

As mentioned previously, Bruckner's *Gloria* does not include the first phrase of text, "*Gloria in excelsis Deo.*" The omission can be attributed to the essentially liturgical character of this Mass, since in an actual church service this phrase would be sung by the celebrant alone. In concert settings these words should certainly be interpolated into the score. Robert Simpson suggests that the phrase be sung by male voices in order to provide contrast to Bruckner's music, which gives the second textual phrase ("*Et in terra pax ...*") to the female singers (Simpson 1946, 32). Such timbral contrasting of male and female voices is in keeping with much of the scoring throughout this Mass.

Bruckner has also provided a hint as to which plainchant *Gloria* should be employed. The melody of the "*Et in terra pax ...,*" in unison and assigned to female voices, is based on the second phrase of *Gloria VIII* from the Roman Catholic liturgy.[11]

Example 5.4A:
E-minor Mass—Gloria—bars 1–7

Et in ter- ra pax ho- mi-   ni–bus bo–nae vo–lun–ta- tis

Example 5.4B:
Gloria VIII—Liber Usualis—p. 37

Et in ter–ra pax homi-   ni- bus

It seems logical that Bruckner would have intended that the first phrase of this plainchant be interpolated into his score, especially since in *Gloria VIII*, unlike virtually all other chants for this section of the Mass, the same melody is used for both the "*Gloria in excelsis ...*"·and the "*Et in terra pax ...*"

These opening bars establish a number of compositional principles that have significance for this movement. Bruckner's plainchant-based, *phrygian* melody, or developments of it, reappear frequently, providing substantial musical unity. The harmony in the opening bars is also modal, alternating between two chords—C major and A minor. Several passages throughout the movement display similar, non directional harmonic sequences of major and relative minor chords. Perhaps most important, the instruments assume an independent role for the first time. In the initial bars the bassoons contribute an energetic, *arpeggiated* figure that provides considerable rhythmic momentum to the unison melody in the female voices, and

---

[11]It is also in *phrygian* mode—an obvious reference to the beginning of the *Kyrie* (Kurth 1971, II: 1222).

is, in effect, a development of it. Voices and bassoons are in unison on every strong beat (Kurth 1971, II: 1222–23). Similar woodwind figures persists in one form or another throughout much of the movement. The accompaniment often functions independently of the choir, adding rhythmic and contrapuntal interest, establishing changes of mood, and reflecting the meaning of the text. Where the instruments double the voices, they do so in order to emphasize important textual phrases and to guide the singers through complex harmonic sequences.

Like the *Kyrie*, this movement is tripartite in structure. Formal divisions are again based on the text, but the words of the *Gloria* separate into three parts in a less obvious way. Bruckner divided the text logically by using the words that refer to humankind, from "*Qui tollis peccata mundi...*" to "*Qui sedes ad dexteram Patris, miserere nobis*," as the basis of the "B" section of his music. The preceding and following verses are directed to God and to Christ, and are set to similar, but not identical, music:

[Gloria in excelsis Deo.]
Et in terra pax hominibus bonae volun-
tatis.
Laudamus te, benedicimus te, adoramus
te, glorificamus te.
Gratias agimus tibi propter magnam glor-
iam tuam.
Domine Deus, Rex coelestis, Deus Pater
omnipotens.
Domine Fili unigenite, Jesu Christe.
Domine Deus, Agnus Dei, Filius Patris.

Qui tollis peccata mundi, miserere nobis.
Qui tollis peccata mundi, suscipe deprecationem nostram.
Qui sedes ad dexteram Patris, miserere
nobis.

Quoniam tu solus sanctus.
Tu solus Dominus.
Tu solus altissimus, Jesu Christe, cum
Sancto Spiritu, in gloria Dei Patris.
Amen.

[Glory to God in the highest]
And on earth peace to men of goodwill.
We praise thee, we bless thee, we adore
thee, we glorify thee.
We give thanks for thy great glory.
Lord God, King of Heaven, God the
Father almighty.
Lord, your only begotten son, Jesus
Christ.
Lord God, Lamb of God, Son of the
Father.

Who takest away the sins of the world,
have mercy upon us.
Who takest away the sins of the world,
hear our prayer.
Thou that sittest at the right hand of the
Father, have mercy upon us.

For Thou only are holy.
Thou only are Lord.
Thou only, O Jesus Christ, with the Holy
Spirit, are most high in the glory of God
the Father.
Amen.

The initial "A" has two sub-sections. In the first Bruckner's plainchant-based melody is extended to comprise four phrases, each of which is designed to illuminate successive images in the text (Simpson 1946, 32). The music expressing "*Et in terra pax ...*" and "*adoramus te*" is quiet and texturally simple, while that depicting "*Laudamus te, benedicimus te*" and "*glorificamus te*" is loud and more complex. Both of these latter phrases are accompanied by rapid, contrary-motion,

note-exchange counterpoint in the instruments, and the "*glorificamus te*" is canonic
as well. These exuberant passages are clearly intended to project the excitement of
all humanity praising God. The ensuing sub-section begins much like its predecessor, but then establishes its own unique ideas. The words "*Domine Deus, Rex
coelestis*" and "*Domine Fili unigenite*" are set as four and five layers of *ostinati*.[12]
Harmonically, these passages recall the opening bars of the movement, swinging
between two chords—major and relative minor. The combination of non directional
harmony with repetitive melodic figuration creates the impression of time standing
still, as if reflecting a wish to repeat forever the name of God and His Son. This
directionless quality is replaced in both instances by astonishing modulations
—from G major to D-flat major at bars 29–39, and from what appears to be B-flat
major to D major during bars 42–53. The initial "A" section ends with a series of
rapid antiphonal responses between choir and wind ensemble that serve as a
transition to the next section, during which *antiphony* will be developed to a high
degree.

The "B" section, with its worldly words, is at a much slower tempo and has
quite a different character. Much of this music is *a capella*, and Bruckner makes
the most of the timbral possibilities within the ensemble by contrasting the male
and female voices with each other and with the full choir, and by setting the brass
instruments against the woodwinds. The transition from section "A" begins the
process of timbral contrast by presenting a sound colour new to this work—two
repetitions of a horn *soli* that is drawn from this composer's early *Cantata: Heil,
Vater! Dir zum hohen Feste.*

Example 5.5A:
E-minor Mass—Gloria—bars 63–65

Example 5.5B:
Cantata: Heil, Vater! ... Feste—Mvt. 1—bars 14–15

The first choral entry, for female voices, is an obvious derivative of the horn

---

[12]In both cases at least one of these *ostinati* is based on the "*Et in terra pax*" theme.

soli, but is also based on a passage from the *Kyrie*.

Example 5.6A:
*E-minor Mass—Gloria—*bars 65–68

Example 5.6B:
*E-minor Mass—Kyrie—*bars 13–16

The words, which plead for Christ's mercy, are reflected in the *a capella* timbre, the female-male *antiphony*, and especially in the harmony. The initial choral passage introduces two distinctive sonorities that colour virtually all the music of this section—the D minor added-sixth chord that appears in bar two of Example 5.6A, and the contrapuntally created chord that follows it. This latter structure is difficult to identify specifically, and functions differently on each of its three appearances.[13] At the words "*suscipe deprecationem nostram ...*" ("receive our prayer ..."), these chords and textures disappear. The choir is united in chorale-style harmonies, the woodwinds add an energetic eighth-note *obbligato*, and a rapid *crescendo* leads to a massive climax. These changes apparently were intended to reflect the hopeful mood implied in this textual fragment (Simpson 1946, 32). Not surprisingly, the original chords and textures return at the final phrase of text —"*miserere nobis.*"

Despite the recurring use of distinctive sonorities, the tonality of this section is in constant flux. The music cadences frequently, but always in different keys, none of which are related in conventional ways.

The use of the instruments is particularly sensitive. Antiphonal sound blocks, either choral or instrumental, are connected to each other by brief instrumental solos that enhance the colour of the scoring as well as bind this section together.

The arrival of the final "A" section is clearly recognizable by the return of previously heard music, but, as he did in the *Kyrie*, Bruckner adapted the form to accommodate his musical ideas. This second "A" is not a simple repeat of material,

---

[13]It functions as an unusually resolved F dominant seventh at its first appearance, as a German sixth substituting for the dominant of A minor at its second, and as an ornamented preparation for an E-flat dominant seventh at its third.

but is, in effect, a harmonic development of a motive from the plainchant-based melody that appeared at the beginning of the *Gloria* (see Example 5.4A). A short woodwind interlude connects the "B" section to the final "A", and re-establishes the initial tempo. During these bars the *arpeggiated* bassoon figure returns and the clarinets introduce the motive that will be the basis of the development to come.

Example 5.7:
E-minor Mass—Gloria—bars 94–97

The musical development of a single important motive may have been suggested to the composer by the parallel structure of the words. Virtually every textual phrase is set to the clarinet motive transposed to different pitch levels. The final statement appears in the horns, initially very quietly (like a memory), but then as part of a huge climactic *crescendo* at the words "*Cum Sancto Spiritu ... Patris.*" Overall, this section is more lightly textured than its counterpart at the beginning of the movement. However, Bruckner reinforces the aural connection between the sections by textural as well as melodic reference. At the end of the first choral passage, clarinets and bassoons hint at the contrary-motion, note-exchange counterpoint that was an important textural element of the initial phrases of the movement.

Two additional musical aspects of this section deserve special mention. At the words "*Jesu Christe,*" the choir is suddenly unaccompanied and in F-sharp major —an unexpected timbre and tonality that are clearly intended to highlight these words. The climactic cadence that follows is equally surprising. A German sixth on A-flat is extended for five full bars, generating enormous tension before resolving to G major.

The "*Amen*" that concludes the movement is a massive double *fugue*. The two subjects are related to each other, but do not have any obvious connection to other material.[14]

Example 5.8:
E-minor Mass—Gloria—bars 133–36 (subjects)

Bruckner does, however, relate this music to the rest of the movement through

---

[14]Interestingly, this *fugue* does not follow the theoretical rules that Bruckner had studied so assiduously during the 1850s. For example, the first two entries of both subjects are at the octave, not the fifth, and subsequent entries also establish unusual relationships. Such deviations from the norm support Bruckner's view that "counterpoint is not genius, but only a means to an end" (Göllerich/Auer 1974, III/1: 382).

his part-writing. Much of the free material throughout the *fugue* consists of cont-rary-motion, note-exchange counterpoint. The instruments participate equally with the choir in the contrapuntal activity, doubling some of the voice lines and carefully highlighting the most important motives. The *fugue* hesitates briefly in E major before initiating a final extended closing that begins as a very close *stretto* on the second *fugue* subject, then broadens out to effect a cadence of symphonic propor-tions in the original key of C major.

Compared to the *Kyrie*, the *Gloria* of the *E-minor Mass* is immeasurably more varied. This is hardly surprising considering the rich imagery of the text, which precipitated new ideas in very rapid succession. However, despite the abundance of concepts and the multiplicity of sudden changes in any of several parameters, the musical flow is never disrupted. Bruckner was able to draw together the diverse elements of this movement by identifying very subtle musical relationships and ensuring that they would be heard.[15] The ultimate result is music that surprises and delights the ear but never disturbs the listener's aesthetic sensibilities.

The two versions of this movement display a number of differences. Some involve minor realignment of text, but, in most cases, single bars in the 1866 ver-sion have been expanded to two bars in the 1882 edition in order to add breadth to transitional passages. These changes probably date from 1876 when Bruckner "structurally tidied up" all three of his great Masses (Nowak 1959, iii). Virtually all of the alterations to the *Gloria* result in enhanced expressivity by permitting or requiring more *rubato* than was indicated in the earlier version. This is perhaps a reflection of the change in Bruckner's status at the time that the revisions were undertaken. By 1876, and certainly by 1882, he was no longer in the employ of the Church, but was a professional composer whose primary focus had shifted from sacred music to the composition of symphonies.

CREDO

Bruckner's *Credo* has the most complex structure and the most diversity of material of any of the movements of the *E-minor Mass*. The text is extensive and is filled with potent imagery, offering bounteous opportunities for tone-painting:

[Credo in unum Deum]
Patrem omnipotentem, Factorem coeli et terrae, visibilium et invisibilium.

[I believe in one God]
The Father Almighty, maker of Heaven and earth, and of all things visible and invisible.

Et in unum Dominum Jesum Christum, Filium Dei unigenitum, et ex Patre natum ante omnia saecula.
Deum de Deo, Lumen de Lumine, Deum

And in one Lord, Jesus Christ, the only-begotten Son of God, and born of the Father before all ages.
God of God, Light of Light, true God of

---

[15]Note, for example, how the brief oboe solos during the "B" section are reflected in the soprano lines that follow them.

verum de Deo vero, genitum non factum, consubstantialem Patri, per quem omnia facta sunt.
Qui propter nos homines, et propter nostram salutem, descendit de coelis.

Et incarnatus est de Spiritu Sancto, ex Maria Virgine, et homo factus est.
Crucifixus etiam pro nobis, sub Pontio Pilato passus et sepultus est.

Et resurrexit tertia die secundum Scripturas, et ascendit in coelum, sedet ad dexteram Patris: et iterum venturus est cum gloria judicare vivos et mortuos, cujus regni non erit finis.

Et in Spiritum Sanctum, Dominum et vivificantem, qui ex Patre Filioque procedit, qui cum Patre et Filio simul adoratur et conglorificatur, qui locutus est per prophetas.
Et unam Sanctam Catholicam et Apostolicam Ecclesiam.
Confiteor unum Baptisma in remissionem peccatorum et expecto resurrectionem mortuorum, et vitam venturi saeculi.
Amen.

true God, begotten not made, consubstantial with the Father, by whom all things were made.
Who for us and for our salvation, came down from Heaven.

And was made incarnate by the Holy Spirit, born of the Virgin Mary, and was made man.
He was crucified for us, suffered under Pontius Pilate, died, and was buried.

And on the third day he rose again according to the Scriptures, and ascended into Heaven, and sitteth on the right hand of the Father: and He shall come again with glory to judge the living and the dead, of whose kingdom there shall be no end.

And in the Holy Spirit, the Lord and giver of life, who proceedeth from the Father and the Son, who together with the Father and the Son is adored and glorified, who spoke through the prophets.
And in one Holy Catholic and Apostolic Church.
I confess one baptism for the remission of sins and I await the resurrection of the dead, and the life of the world to come.
Amen.

The composer's approach to the division of the text is not especially unusual. The first two verses, "*Credo in unum Deum ... invisiblium*" and "*Et in unum Dominum Jesum Christum ... descendit de coelis*," employ the same music. The "*Et incarnatus est ...*" precipitates new and highly contrasting material. The music for the "*Et resurrexit ...*" provides additional contrast, although, as will be seen, this section is related to earlier material. The final section "*Et in Spiritum Sanctum ...*" repeats the music from the beginning of the movement. The overall structure, A-B-C-A, can be found in *Credo* movements by many composers; however, Bruckner fills this form with highly individual ideas that bind the movement together and connect it to other parts of this Mass.

Like the *Gloria*, this movement does not include the first phrase of text ("*Credo in unum Deum*"). This phrase, intoned in the style of plainsong, should certainly precede the first written music, but Bruckner has provided no hint as to which chant should be used. The opening phrases are in unison and have the character of plainchant, but do not conform to any of the six chants specified for the *Credo* in the Roman Catholic liturgy. However, *Credo I, II,* and *IV* set the "*Credo in unum Deum*" to the same melody, and *Credo I* is identified as the "authentic tone" for these words (*Liber Usualis* 1952, 66). It seems reasonable then that the first phrase of *Credo I* should be interpolated into Bruckner's Mass.

Example 5.9:
Credo I—Liber Usualis—p. 64

From the beginning a significant relationship is established between the chorus and the wind ensemble. The main theme of the movement, presented in the first four bars, consists of a descending sequence in which choir and woodwinds, both in unison, alternate on the repetitions of the sequenced motive. These four bars, or derivatives of them, reappear frequently throughout the "A" sections, and provide material for other sections as well.[16]

Example 5.10:
E-minor Mass—Credo—bars 1–5

When setting a text expressing belief in one God, unison writing is often an important symbol. Bruckner makes extensive use of unison textures in his music for the first, second and last verses, and also incorporates *ostinati* as another means of reflecting the steadfastness of Christian Faith. The rapid tempo and brisk surface rhythms of these sections permit him to enunciate large amounts of text very quickly. The entire text of the first stanza is pronounced in eight bars.

The transition from verse one to verse two is accomplished with great skill. At the words "*visibilium ... invisibilium*" the music breaks into harmony. The chords presented are the supertonic, subdominant, and German sixth in the tonic—C major. The voices stop on the German sixth, but the music is continued by a short brass fanfare that presents a startlingly dissonant sonority—a chord built in fifths —that fades into a $V^7 \rightarrow I$ cadence in C major. The cadence elides with the beginning of the second verse ("*Et in unum Dominum ...*"), which repeats exactly

---

[16]This motive has a curious affinity with the *Scherzo* of *Symphony No. 8* (Simpson 1946, 33).

the first two bars of the movement.[17] This clever writing allows Bruckner to ac-
complish three things at once. He is able to reflect the meaning of the words, signal
the beginning of a new textual stanza by changing the timbre, and fulfil all the
obligations of his harmonic progression without interrupting the flow of the music.

A number of other examples of poetic realization of text appear throughout the
initial "A" section. After several bars of a unison ascending sequence, the music
arrives on an F-sharp major chord at the words "*lumen de lumine.*" Bruckner
frequently uses such "bright" keys to project images of light.[18] The ensuing words
"*Deum verum de Deo vero*" are set to a conventional cadence in D minor, an
apparent use of harmonic stability to reflect the "trueness" of God. An *ostinato* in
D minor on the main theme of the movement comprises the next several phrases.
The repetition of material is undoubtedly a metaphor for the consubstantiality of
Father and Son; that is, they are made of the same material. At the conclusion of
the *ostinato*, the D minor harmony is replaced by E-flat major—another example
of the Neapolitan harmonic relationship much favoured by Bruckner[19]—and a
subtle way of drawing attention to the words "*omnia facta sunt.*" This verse
concludes with the words "*descendit de coelis,*" set to a descending *arpeggio* of an
E diminished-seventh chord. The bassoons continue this line, as the texture thins
and the tempo slows to prepare for the "B" section.

The "B" section contrasts strongly with its predecessor. Much of this section
is *a capella*, the tempo is *adagio*, and, for the most part, unison textures have
disappeared. The influence of Palestrina is again apparent, since the choral writing
is canonic and antiphonal. Third-related chords give the harmony of the "*Et incarnatus est*" a modal feeling, an effect that is reinforced in the 1882 version by tonally ambiguous cadences on open fifths. However, despite the obvious contrast
with previous music, the melodic ideas are derived from the main theme of the
movement, another masterstroke of musical unity.

The "*Crucifixus*" is very gentle and heartfelt. The choral parts consist of a
simple chorale in F minor,[20] and are accompanied by a countermelody in the horns

---

[17]The appearance of harmony at this point was probably intended to reflect the fact that
the text is plural—"all things visible and invisible." Setting the word "*invisibilium*" as a
German sixth is likely another poetic idea—an unresolved chord illustrating a mystical
concept.

[18]See, for example, the second movement of *Germanenzug* at the words "*ist es licht.*"

[19]Another striking example of the Neapolitan relationship appears at bars 104–5 of the
1882 version of this movement. The mid-point of the phrase that sets the words "*secundum
scripturas*" displays the progression AM → B♭M → AM. This progression does not appear
in the 1866 edition.

[20]This chorale is harmonized differently in the two versions. While the phrases in the
1866 version always cadence on the tonic, those of the later version tend toward the
dominant.

and a syncopated, unison *obbligato* in clarinets and bassoons that adds rhythmic momentum to the choral textures and immeasurably heightens the expressivity of the passage. The *obbligato* continues through the next few phrases, which recall the "*Et incarnatus est*," but in F minor like the "*Crucifixus*." The words "*passus, et sepultus est*" are portrayed by music from the "*Crucifixus*" that gets gradually quieter and lower in register. The burial of Christ is further "depicted" by an instrumental interlude consisting of quiet descending chords. This interlude is scored differently in the two versions, but both are effective. In the original version these chords are assigned to low-register oboes and solo clarinet. The revised version entrusts them to the trombones, a tone colour that enhances their solemnity.

Not surprisingly, the words of the "C" section, which deal with the resurrection, inspired a significant change in the music. The sombre harmony that illustrated the burial of Christ is replaced by pulsating chords in the lowest register of bassoons and clarinets that reestablish the rapid tempo, and, since they gradually ascend, seem to represent "new life rising from the depths" (Simpson 1946, 34). Although the musical material presented here is new, the antiphonal texture of the choral writing and the energetic woodwind *obbligato* connect this segment to earlier music.

All of the music of this section is exuberant. Bruckner constantly varies the woodwind *obbligato* to generate more energy, and the brass are employed extensively. Their use is certainly pictorial—fanfares accompanying Christ's resurrection —and other examples of tone-painting appear as well. The words "*et ascendit in coelum*" are presented as a D major scale that sweeps upward, a long-range answer to the descending *arpeggio* that was matched to "*descendit de coelis*" earlier in the movement. Immediately following the words "*cum gloria*," the music recalls the beginning of the *Gloria* of this Mass, an example of self-referential tone-painting and an expert stroke of musical integration. This recalling of previous material also has symbolic meaning. Setting the "*Judicare*" to the same music as the "*Et in terra pax ...*" indicates that Christ's judgment on Doomsday brings to the earth the peace and goodwill that is so fervently wished for in the text of the *Gloria* (Göllerich/- Auer 1974, III/1: 388). The ensuing phrase, "*cujus regni non erit finis*," is set entirely in unresolved dominant-seventh and augmented-sixth chords symbolizing the unending character of God's kingdom. These bars subtly prepare the return of the "A" section. As he had between the first and second stanzas of this text, Bruckner uses a brief brass fanfare to resolve the German-sixth chord in C on the last syllable of "*finis*" by presenting a $V^7 \rightarrow I$ cadence in the original tonic.

The final "A" section begins by recalling exactly the initial bars of the movement. Generally, the structure of this section follows that of the initial "A"; however, Bruckner uses the woodwind *obbligato* to recall motives from other parts of the movement, and he introduces some striking new ideas. For example, when the music breaks into harmony at the fifth bar, all resemblance to the opening sounds vanishes in an astonishing progression that accomplishes an abrupt modulation from F major to E major.

Example 5.11:
E-minor Mass—Credo—bars 159–62

A distinctive two-voice choral texture appears at the words "*Confiteor unum baptisma.*" These bars are a slightly altered recapitulation of the *ostinato* at the words "*genitum non factum ... Patri,*" and have a similar poetic purpose—the reflection of the concept of oneness. The choral texture, however, is unlike any other in this work.

Bruckner chose to separate the word "*mortuorum*" from the rest of the text. He set it *a capella* and at a slower tempo in a passage that recalls the *Kyrie* of this Mass.

Example 5.12A:
E-minor Mass—Credo—bars 205–10

Example 5.12B:
E-minor Mass—Kyrie—bars 4–6

The final textual phrase is a vision of paradise. In setting these words Bruckner drew on ideas from earlier in the movement, and combined them in a way that reflects an important religious principle. Pulsating low-register chords in clarinets and bassoons (new life out of death again), and antiphonal choral writing connect this segment to the "*Resurrexit.*" However, the melodic material is a canonic version of the main theme, and is very similar in texture to the "*Et incarnatus est.*" Christ's incarnation as a human, his resurrection, and the prospect of eternal life for

all humanity is an intellectual principle central to Christian belief, and was profoundly important to Bruckner. It is hardly surprising, then, that he would draw
these ideas together musically when setting this text (Kurth 1971, II: 1231). The
imitative textures become homophonic at the "*Amen*," and the music broadens out
into a grand, but conventionally harmonized, cadence.

The scoring of this final cadence is quite different in the two versions of the
movement. In the 1866 setting the homophonic "*Amen*" is enlivened by another
derivation of the main theme played by the trombones. The trombone *soli* does not
appear in the 1882 version, which seems unfortunate, since it adds considerable
energy to these closing bars. One wonders if perhaps Bruckner ultimately felt that
this passage was too "symphonic" for a religious composition. The original cadence
unquestionably does have symphonic proportions.

Bruckner's *Credo* is a work of immense vigour and confidence. The assuredness of the music is certainly a reflection of the composer's commitment to the
Roman Catholic liturgy, and constitutes a personal statement of Faith. It is also
amazingly imaginative. More than any other music in this Mass, the *Credo* demonstrates the poetic nature of Bruckner's mind. Examples of tone-painting abound,
and, considering the multitude of distinctive ideas, it seems astonishing that the
composer could unify them in such a remarkably skilful way.

As implied in the preceding annotation, there are substantial differences
between the two versions of this movement. Like previous movements, many
transitional passages are recomposed, and most are extended to smooth the connections from idea to idea. However, a number of other important alterations
appear that have not been previously seen, at least not to this degree. Two notable
changes in scoring have already been discussed, but much of the music is rescored,
primarily by rearranging the parts among the instruments. A substantial number of
revisions to the harmonic structure occur. Most of these clarify the harmony at
transitions, but others considerably alter the effect of several passages—especially
the "*Et incarnatus est*" and the "*Crucifixus*." Melodic and rhythmic revisions also
have a profound effect on the "*Et incarnatus est*," but appear in other places as
well. Overall, the 1882 version is fourteen bars longer than its predecessor and generally shows the increased proficiency that its composer had developed in the
sixteen years that had elapsed between the creation of the original and the revised
versions. However, in his efforts to create a more seamless composition, Bruckner
smoothed out the edges of some truly remarkable harmony.

SANCTUS

Like the *Kyrie*, the text for this movement offers little opportunity for tone-
painting. Bruckner's setting draws primarily on musical rather than poetic means,
although certain aspects of the climactic passages can be taken to have metaphoric
intent:

Sanctus, sanctus, sanctus,	Holy, holy, holy,
Dominus Deus Sabaoth,	Lord God of Hosts,

Pleni sunt coeli et terra gloria tua,   Heaven and earth are filled with Thy
Hosanna in excelsis.   glory,
                                                Hosanna in the highest.

In his music for the *Sanctus*, Bruckner again turned to sixteenth-century models. The first part of this relatively short movement is based on a motive from Palestrina's *Missa brevis*, which is used to construct a magnificent *a capella* polyphonic chorus in eight voices that is clearly indebted to the Italian Renaissance master.

Example 5.13A:
Palestrina—*Missa brevis—Sanctus*—bars 1–4

Example 5.13B:
***E-minor Mass—Sanctus*—bars 1–4**

The motive appears in close canon at the fifth initially in alto I and tenor I, but progresses through pairs of voices until it has been presented by all eight parts. Bruckner surrounds these canons with other free-flowing counterpoint, much of which consists of fragments or derivatives of the main motive. The complex texture that ensues conceals the primary melodic material much of the time (Simpson 1946, 34), but, since many of the additional lines are closely related, the chorus is tightly unified. The restrained dynamic gives this music an intimate quality, "as if the Lord was close by," and the multitude of musical lines creates the illusion of hundreds of voices (Göllerich/Auer 1974, III/1: 389).

The polyphonic texture disappears abruptly at the first climax, which occurs at the words "*Dominus Deus Sabaoth*." These words are declaimed at triple *forte* by the chorus and the low brass using a single chord—a D dominant-seventh. The rhythm is based on the speech pattern of the words.

The passage following this climax is radically different in the two versions of the Mass. In the original version a five-bar interlude appears, during which the woodwinds present a four-voice canon based on the descending scale from the end of the principal motive, and the female voices contribute a unison melody in rising fourths. In the 1882 edition the woodwind canon is reduced to two bars, and the vocal melody is removed altogether. Since the ensuing passage ("*Pleni sunt coeli ...*") is the major climax of the movement, these alterations have a dramatically different effect. In the original version the second climax arrives rather slowly, prepared by the increasing complexity of the imitative woodwind writing, and by the rising choral melody. No such preparation exists in the later setting. The second climactic passage appears suddenly, displacing the woodwind canon almost before it can be established, and certainly enhancing the intensity of these bars.

At the main climax the choral textures are again homophonic. The choir sings in block chords and presents a non tonal progression with roots that descend by fifths. This section is connected to earlier music by the trombones and low horns, which reiterate the primary motive in close canon at the fifth just as it appeared in the initial bars of the movement. The towering chords that appear here were inspired by the words, "*Pleni sunt coeli ... tua.*" These huge choral blocks, spread over two-and-one-half octaves, are a symbolic representation of God's massive grandeur, and a graphic depiction of His glory, filling all of Heaven and earth. The score demands that the intensity of these bars be sustained until the end of the movement, and during this time several interesting ideas emerge.

Example 5.14A:
E-minor Mass—Sanctus—bars 36–37 (voices only)

Example 5.14B:
E-minor Mass—Credo—bar 39

Example 5.14C:
E-minor Mass—Credo—bars 122–24 (voices only)

At the word "*gloria,*" the voices become unison and recall the previous movement. The motive articulated here is the retrograde of the unison figure that accompanied the word "*omnia*" in the *Credo*, but is also a reminiscence of the "*cum gloria*" from later in that same movement.[21]

Bruckner separated the "*Hosanna*" from the "*in excelsis*," and the intervening bars are again differentiated between the versions. In the 1866 setting the separation consists of a single bar, which is filled by the trombones playing a fragment from the primary motive. In the revised version this interlude is expanded to three bars, and the trombone figuration is extended and less precisely linked to earlier material.

Bruckner's *Sanctus* is in many ways the crown of the Mass as a whole. In this composition he shows himself to be a master of contrapuntal writing, and of the ability to plan, create, and sustain a dramatic climax. Although this magnificent music is grounded in the past, it also illustrates the growth in Bruckner's symphonic thought—a development that was to absorb his talents more and more in the future.

The most important differences between the two versions have already been discussed. However, the *Sanctus* is another movement in which Bruckner changed the meter signature from *alla breve* to common time. He wanted this movement to be taken at a slow tempo—a performance challenge that has always been problematic. After the Linz premiere of the revised version on October 4, 1885, the conductor, Adalbert Schreyer, wrote:

Bruckner could have wished the *Sanctus*, which opens with an unaccompanied polyphonic passage in the manner of Palestrina, rather slower, though he was forced to admit that I had good reasons, for instance the loss of pitch, for not taking it any slower (Nowak 1959, iii).

Through the years conductors have generally agreed with Schreyer, and have found it difficult to maintain both pitch and *legato* if the movement is conducted in four (Hillis 1991, 89). The pulse in this music simply *is* at the half bar, precisely as Bruckner conceived it in the original version.

BENEDICTUS

In the *Benedictus*[22] many of the stylistic principles that appeared in earlier movements are continued and developed, but a number of new concepts are introduced as well. Much of the writing again draws on archaic models. Choral *antiphony* similar to that seen in previous movements recurs, and responsive textures, reminiscent of the Venetian style of Giovanni Gabraeli among others, appear for the first time. The harmony, however, is Bruckner's own, and is fully representative

---

[21]Such self-referencing has been previously noted in this chapter, and is typical of Bruckner's approach to musical unity.

[22]This movement offers the only alternative instrumentation in the entire work. Bruckner suggests that the oboes might be replaced by an additional pair of clarinets. Substituting the lyrical clarinet sound for the more pungent oboe timbre is in keeping with the introspective character of this music, but it seems unlikely that most conductors would avail themselves of this possibility.

of the nineteenth-century. The movement is formally surprising, since it is cast in sonata form—a highly unusual occurrence in a Mass.

In keeping with the words, the mood is subdued, even awestruck. Since this text offers little in the way of imagery, nothing in this movement is represented pictorially. The music expresses the religious mystery behind the words, and projects both an intimate, personal view, and a broad, universal understanding of the meaning of Christ's ultimate sacrifice:

Benedictus qui venit in nomine Domine,   Blessed is he that cometh in the name of
Hosanna in excelsis.   the Lord,
                                              Hosanna in the highest.

The primary theme is presented by solo horn, and is accompanied by an important counterpoint in the sopranos.

Example 5.15:
E-minor Mass—Benedictus—bars 1–8

This theme and its counterpoint immediately connect this movement to earlier music. The half-step lower-neighbour figure is derived from the motive that provided most of the imitation in the *Kyrie* (see Example 5.2), and the soprano line recalls the oboe solo from the "*Qui tollis ...*" of the *Gloria*.

Example 5.16:
E-minor Mass—Gloria—bars 95–98

The descending octave that concludes the horn theme is similar to many other melodic structures in this Mass, and in Bruckner's music generally, but listeners would probably relate it most readily to the *Hosanna* of the *Sanctus*, which occurs a few bars before the conclusion of the previous movement.

Example 5.17:
E-minor Mass—Sanctus—bars 40–41 (unison voices)

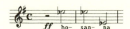

However, the opening harmonic/melodic structure was also influenced by another source. Bruckner heard Wagner's *Tristan und Isolde* in Munich in May 1865 and had prepared for this event by studying the score (Watson 1977, 21). The horn melody with its three rising semi-tones, and the harmony of the initial two bars are clearly inspired by the revolutionary opening of the *Tristan* prelude (Redlich 1955, 73).

Example 5.18A:
E-minor Mass—Benedictus—bars 1–2

Example 5.18B:
Wagner—*Tristan—Prelude*—bars 2–3

The chordal structure of the first eight bars is very chromatic, making a precise definition of the tonality difficult—another *Tristan* influence—but the key appears to be C major. After these introductory bars, the choir becomes antiphonal, and the harmony is significantly clearer. These bars, which serve as a transition, provide contrast and modulate to the dominant to prepare for the entry of the secondary theme, which is, in fact, the primary theme in the secondary key.

The development introduces a number of interesting ideas. The choral textures are consistently antiphonal or responsive, generating complex harmonies, some of which are related by thirds. Fragments from the primary theme are embedded in the counterpoint and appear in virtually every bar, but Bruckner also generated a new motive that is developed canonically during the first part of this section. Throughout the development and recapitulation, the woodwinds weave a rapid, largely single-line filigree around the chorus, generating some of the most demanding instrumental writing in the entire work. The entrance of the recapitulation (bar 61) is obscured by this woodwind *obbligato*, and the arrival of the primary theme is further disguised by appearing quietly in the lowest registers of horn and bassoon. The primary theme and the transition are restated much as they appeared during the exposition, but are decorated by the woodwind filigree, and the *antiphony* is reversed between the male and female choruses. The recapitulation elides into a brief coda (bar 79) based on the development motive, and culminating in an exultant climax at the words "*hosanna in excelsis.*"

The *Benedictus* contains some of the most lyrical music of the entire work. Loud dynamics are sparingly employed and very loud volume levels are reserved for final "*hosanna ....*" For the most part, choral lines follow smooth profiles. The bass voices near the beginning of the development, with their numerous leaps of fifths and octaves, are a notable exception, and may be regarded as an anticipation of the ensuing movement when such angular writing has poetic intent.

The two versions display numerous differences in the details of the harmony, rhythm, and scoring. As has been observed rather consistently throughout earlier movements, in the revised version many transitions are extended from one to two bars, affording a smoother flow from section to section. In the *Benedictus* Bruckner added sustained chords in the trombones that bridge the gap between phrases and guide the pitch of the choir. In this movement the additional bars also provide a clearer definition of the structural elements. However, the major revision involves the primary theme. In the 1882 version, this theme is extended by one bar, which adds to the chromaticism of the melody itself and has obvious implications for the secondary theme and the recapitulation.

AGNUS DEI

The *Agnus Dei* contains some of the most heartfelt and forward-looking music in the entire work. Bruckner goes to considerable lengths to create ethereal, other-worldly textures, and the dissonance of some of the harmony is truly astonishing. This movement also illustrates a long-range structural principle that was very common at the time. The nineteenth-century interest in cyclic forms is reflected in many masses by setting the *Agnus Dei* to the same music as the *Kyrie*. Bruckner acknowledges this tradition in the *E-minor Mass*, but, as will be seen, his recalling of material from the *Kyrie* is both unorthodox and subtle. Also, as has been the case throughout this work, the *Agnus* contains hints of other movements as well.

This movement has a tripartite structure that is created by repeating the first of the two lines of text:

Agnus Dei, qui tollis peccata mundi: Miserere nobis.	Lamb of God, who takest away the sins of the world: Have mercy on us.
Agnus Dei ... nobis.	Lamb of God ... us.
Agnus Dei, qui tollis peccata mundi: Dona nobis pacem.	Lamb of God, who takest away the sins of the world: Grant us peace.

All three sections use the same musical material, but none of them simply repeat earlier music. Each section presents a transformed version of the melodic, harmonic, and textural elements appearing at the beginning of the movement.

At first glance this text seems to offer little opportunity for pictorial representation. However, Bruckner creates a number of passages that musically depict his understanding of these words, and several of them are quite graphic. At its first appearance (bar 5–6) the word "*mundi*" is harmonized by a D-sharp diminished ninth chord resolving to E minor. The "dark" sound of these bars seems to portray a world burdened with sin. When this word returns in the second section of the movement and after the first "*miserere*" (bars 25–26), the chord progression is much brighter (Am^7 → FM → CV^7), as if the mercy of Christ had already lifted some of the world's darkness.

In each of the first two sections, the words "*miserere nobis*" appear twice in different settings. The initial appearance in each section is as a large block of eight-voice, imitative polyphony. Numerous suspensions create a harmonic context filled with sharp dissonance that increases in intensity as the passages progress toward their climaxes. At the high point of the first block (bar 12), a quadruple suspension results in a sonority that includes every pitch of a G major scale sounding simultaneously. The second block is two bars longer than the first, and the most dissonant sonority is reached at bar 35 in a polychord consisting of complete A-flat major and E-flat major triads. These massive structures represent the whole world imploring Christ for mercy (Simpson 1946, 35), and the poignancy of these passages is enhanced by the bass voices, which present a series of wide leaps over octaves or tenths [23] (Watson 1977, 98). However, they are also a graphic depiction of the sound of voices within a large cathedral. As would be heard within the reverberant acoustic of such a large space, the voices overlap and resonate *en masse* to create a blended, vibrant sound that mixes together the pitches of adjacent chords. All church musicians would have been familiar with this sound, but no one prior to Bruckner had attempted to replicate it in an actual composition.

The movement begins with a unison choral phrase that initially is reminiscent of plainsong, but later recalls the chromaticism of the horn theme from the *Benedictus*. To this, Bruckner added only a unison *obbligato* in woodwinds. The woodwind line is sequential in construction and makes a clear reference to the *Gloria*.

Example 5.19:
E-minor Mass—Gloria—bars 19–21

Example 5.20:
E-minor Mass—Agnus—bars 1–6

---

[23]This melodic structure was anticipated by the bass voices in the *Benedictus*.

As previously observed, the music breaks into harmony at the word "*mundi*," which leads directly to the first polyphonic "*miserere*."[24] A brass fanfare crowns the climax of this passage, and the section is concluded by another "*miserere*." Subdued and antiphonal, this second statement pits the female voices against the male singers. The choral lines are all derived from the opening bars of the movement. While the antiphonal texture suggests a congregation, the reserved, intimate character implies a personal prayer. An instrumental interlude comprising a bassoon solo accompanied by descending chromatic lines in two horns leads to the next section.

The second section begins exactly like the first, except that the choral and woodwind lines are transposed up a perfect fifth. As noted earlier, the cadence at the word "*mundi*" is drawn in lighter colours than in the previous section, as if Christ's mercy has already been effected. The ensuing polyphonic "*miserere*" is longer and somewhat less dissonant than its predecessor. Its climax is crowned by the same brass fanfare that appeared in the first section. The quiet "*miserere*" that follows is called a "prostration" by Simpson (Simpson 1946, 35), and consists of new material. The melody is "hidden" in the inner voices.

Example 5.21:
E-minor Mass—Agnus—bars 36–43

The third section is introduced by a clarinet solo. This final section of the movement employs familiar material that is transformed in many ways.

Example 5.22:
E-minor Mass—Agnus—bars 45–48

---

[24]The dissonances and the *phrygian* harmony of the first *miserere* relate it to the opening of the *Kyrie* (Göllerich/Auer 1974, III/1: 394).

The initial line in female voices is closest to previously heard material since it is an extended version of the unison choral melody from the first bars of the movement. The male voice counterpoint to this melody is directly derived from it. The woodwind *obbligato* is an ornamented version of that which appeared at the beginning of the *Agnus*. This opening passage concludes in a cadence that has long-range structural significance. The choral lines join in a unison motive that is a restatement of the most important canonic subject of the *Kyrie* (see Example 5.2), and, at the same time, the woodwinds present a rhythmically faster version of the same motive.

Example 5.23:
E-minor Mass—Agnus—bars 51–53

The woodwind lines from this point to the end of the work are all repetitions of this motive, and, when the bassoons are placed in canon against oboes/clarinets, textures from the *Kyrie* are also recalled.

The choral writing also echoes that of the first movement.

Example 5.24A:
E-minor Mass—Agnus—bars 53–56

Example 5.24B:
E-minor Mass—Kyrie—bars 29–32

The first two statements of the "*dona nobis pacem*" are whispered by the choir in eight-voice, homophonic textures that are a transformed version of part of the *Kyrie*. In fact, the initial motive of the choral unison from the first bars of the *Agnus* is a retrograde of the soprano melody from the beginning of the *Kyrie*.

Example 5.25A:
E-minor Mass—Agnus—bars 1–2

Example 5.25B:
E-minor Mass—Kyrie—bars 4–6

Since, as has been already noted, this choral unison provides the material for virtually every segment of this movement, it seems appropriate to view the entire *Agnus* as a transformed version of the *Kyrie*.

The final bars of the work are a coda with an ethereal quality that suggests transcendence from this world altogether. The word "*dona*" is set twice in vii^{07} → i cadences in F-sharp minor and A minor. In each case the diminished seventh chord is divided into its component tritones, which oppose each other in contrary motion. The minor chord resolution is similarly structured.

Example 5.26:
E-minor Mass—Agnus—bars 61–62

In the 1882 version Bruckner enhanced the otherworldly character of these bars by asking the male voices to sing *mezza voce* at the first cadence and *falsetto* at the second. The female singers are marked *mezza voce* at the second cadence. At the same time the woodwinds move to the forefront of the texture, ensuring that their *Kyrie* reference will be heard. The wonderful final cadence is marked by a dramatic fade from A major to A minor at its climax, then a long E major triad dissolves the music into silence. As Leopold Nowak has said, "music assumes the stature of prayer" (Nowak 1959, iv).

Differences between the versions are relatively few. Near the beginning the revisions involve rather minor changes in scoring and some clarifications of the harmony; however, later in this movement these emendations assume considerable significance for performance. A bar is added at two crucial points—the climax of the second polyphonic "*miserere*," which makes for a more convincing climax, and at the end of the movement, which permits a more effective *decrescendo* to silence on the final E major chord. During the final section of the movement, the wood-wind lines are rescored to reinforce the relationship to the *Kyrie*, and the extra timbral directions in the choral parts add significantly to the ethereal character of the coda.

The *Mass in E Minor* is a work of inspiration, individuality, and impeccable craftsmanship. With this composition Bruckner, long the master of the older church styles, successfully blended his own particular approach to harmony and counter-point with the earlier liturgical traditions he so admired. This work, with its curious ability to capture the compositional ethic of past, present, and future, stands alone among the sacred works of the nineteenth-century.

The *E-minor Mass* occupies a unique position in nineteenth- and even twentieth-century church music... The writing is ... unusual; a "Palestrina" style and a distinctly modern wind accompaniment to the forceful, even dramatic, choral passages are blended into such a degree of homogeneity that the Mass can claim to be the most essentially ecclesiastical example of its kind. It must be regarded as an intensification of the classical Viennese style to match the profounder sentiments postulated by the liturgy... The originality with which the Linz Cathedral and parish organist set the words of the Mass to music is nothing short of astonishing (Nowak 1977, iii).

Chapter 6

Vienna: "A Tonal Anti-Christ" 1868–96

During the summer of 1868, Bruckner moved to Vienna. He had been attempting to relocate for a number of years and had made several attempts to secure an appointment in the Austrian capital. As early as 1862 he had applied for the position of organist-designate at the Imperial Court Chapel (the *Hofkapelle*). In August, 1867, he petitioned Vienna University for a lectureship in harmony and counterpoint, and reapplied to the *Hofkapelle*. Both applications were rejected, but in September of the same year, his mentor, Simon Sechter, died and the prestigious professorship in harmony and counterpoint at the Vienna Conservatory became available. Despite strong support from Herbeck and Rudolf Weinwurm, it took some time for this appointment to be confirmed. Part of the delay originated with Bruckner himself, who was concerned that the salary being offered was considerably lower than his income in Linz. By Easter 1868 Herbeck had managed to get the salary at the Conservatory increased substantially, and had arranged for Bruckner to be appointed organist-designate at the Imperial Court Chapel. As he had done when leaving St. Florian thirteen years earlier, Bruckner exacted a promise from Bishop Rudigier that his position in Linz would be held open for two years (Watson 1977, 20, 23–24), but on July 23, 1868, he finally accepted the Vienna appointments (Redlich 1955, 15).

As it had been in Linz, Bruckner's life in Vienna was hectic. In addition to his duties at the Conservatory and the *Hofkapelle*, he taught at the teacher-training college of St. Anna, and, in 1875, was appointed to a lectureship in harmony and counterpoint at Vienna University—a post he had coveted for some time. He also took private pupils (Schönzeler 1970, 51–52, 54, 70). Bruckner apparently enjoyed teaching, and there is substantial evidence that his students liked and respected him. His classes included a number of young musicians who would make a significant mark on the profession in the ensuing years. Among his first students at the Conservatory were the conductor Felix Mottl and the musicologist Guido Adler. Later classes included conductors Arthur Nikisch and Emil Paur, the composer

Friedrich Klose, and the organist Hans Rott (Watson 1977, 25–26). Gustav Mahler and Hugo Wolf were both students at the Conservatory during the 1870s and both later became associates but were never actually Bruckner's pupils (Redlich 1955, 114–17). Other notable students were the Schalk brothers, Franz and Joseph, and Ferdinand Löwe. These three men became ardent admirers and, for better and for worse, remained friends, advisors, and advocates for the rest of the composer's life.[1]

Bruckner's Vienna years were marked by a number of awards and accomplishments that reflected his growing recognition within Austria and abroad, but during this time he was also presented with many of his worst disappointments and subjected to savage criticism. On the positive side, his skill as a performer was recognized soon after his arrival in Vienna. In April 1869 he was invited to France to give a series of organ recitals in Nancy and in Paris. He was acclaimed in both venues. Two years later he achieved similar results when he represented Austria at a festival of leading organists in London. Closer to home some of his compositions were achieving success. The Fourth Symphony was very well received at its premiere in Vienna in February 1881, as was the Seventh in December 1884 in Leipzig, and the Eighth in mid-December 1892 in Vienna (Watson 1977, 27–28, 38, 41, 46). The *Symphony No. 7* represented Bruckner's first international success as a symphonist, receiving no fewer than thirty-two performances all over Europe (as well as three in the United States) during his lifetime (Schönzeler 1970, 84–85). Several personal awards were also conferred upon him. In June 1886 he received the Order of Franz Joseph,[2] and in November 1891 the University of Vienna awarded him an honourary doctorate[3]—a tribute that meant an enormous amount to him (Watson 1977, 42, 46).

Mixed among these triumphs were a comparable number of disappointments. His early symphonies were summarily dismissed by Viennese conductors, and the Philharmonic ridiculed the *Symphony No. 2*, calling it the "*Pausensinfonie*" be-

---

[1]These men undoubtedly helped Bruckner to develop his symphonic style during the last decades of the nineteenth century, and were unfailing champions of his music at a time when few people were listening. However, they also pressured Bruckner into tempering many of his most imaginative ideas, and often simply revised his symphonies themselves. Many of the first published editions of the symphonies contained their revisions, which were not always sanctioned by Bruckner, and certainly were not representative of his intentions. Perhaps the best example is the *Symphony No. 9*, which was substantially revised, then performed and published by Löwe. History has discredited these early editions (Doernberg 1960, 113–22).

[2]The Emperor seems to have recognized Bruckner's importance since he contributed personally to the costs of publishing several of the composer's scores. The Eighth Symphony is, of course, dedicated to him.

[3]This event gave rise to the famous incident in which Adolf Exner, the rector of the university, ended his address with the words, "I, *Rector Magnificus* of the University of Vienna, bow before the former assistant teacher of Windhaag" (Doernberg 1960, 107).

cause of its numerous *fermatas*. The premiere of the Third Symphony, on December 16, 1877, was a disaster. The orchestra was hostile and most of the audience had left long before the completion of the performance. Bruckner was so devastated by this event that he virtually ceased composing for a year. Joseph Hellmesberger, *Kapellmeister* to the Emperor and the leader of a fine string quartet, requested a string chamber work from Bruckner in 1878, but then steadfastly refused to perform the composition provided, the *String Quintet in F*, for fear of alienating Viennese audiences. Wagner's death in February 1883 was an enormous blow. However, the greatest disappointment of his compositional life came in September 1887 when the conductor Hermann Levi declared that he could not understand the Eighth Symphony. Levi, whom Bruckner counted among his friends, had actively championed the *Symphony No. 7*, and had been especially selected by the composer to be the first person to see the completed Eighth. Levi's rejection of this monumental work threw Bruckner into despair. He began to doubt his abilities and launched into a period of extensive revisions of his earlier works that, in fact, meant that he would not complete another symphony (Watson 1977, 27, 36, 43–44, 73).

Through all of these incidents, there remained the unrelenting attacks of the critics. The musical press in Vienna, led by Eduard Hanslick, had a decidedly conservative view. Hanslick himself was especially opposed to the so-called "New German School" represented by Wagner and Liszt. He initially supported Bruckner's appointment to the Vienna Conservatory, and had been largely responsible for his being invited to France in April 1869. However, it was Bruckner's very-public admiration of Wagner and especially his *Symphony No. 3*, with its dedication to Wagner,[4] that galvanized Hanslick's opposition to him. Throughout Bruckner's years in Vienna, Hanslick led the chorus of scathing reviews that followed virtually every appearance of a new composition. Other critics generally followed his lead; after a performance of the *String Quintet in F*, one writer called Bruckner "the greatest living musical peril, a sort of tonal anti-Christ" (Watson 1977, 40). Hanslick was also capable of going his own way against the general view. When the *Symphony No. 8* was premiered in Vienna on December 18, 1892, it was acclaimed by the audience and by all the critics save Hanslick, who wrote of its "dream-disturbed, cat's misery style". (Watson 1977, 46).

A century later such comments seem ridiculous, but at the time they caused Bruckner much pain and fed his well-developed insecurities. He was so afraid of Hanslick's attacks that he requested that the Philharmonic refrain from mounting his Seventh Symphony during their 1885–86 season because he was convinced that Hanslick would savage it, and that a bad review in Vienna would affect the popularity the work was achieving outside Austria. When the Philharmonic performed it in March 1886, the audience gave Bruckner an enormous ovation, but, just as he

---

[4]Bruckner always referred to this symphony as his "Wagner Symphony," and the original version contained several direct quotations from Wagner's works. The quotations were removed during the first revision (Schönzeler 1970, 171).

had feared, Hanslick was unimpressed (Schönzeler 1970, 86–87). His venomous rejection of this great work sounds mean-spirited today.[5]

Bruckner's Vienna years were dedicated almost exclusively to the composition and revision of symphonies. Only two large-scale, non symphonic works date from these years—the *Te Deum* of 1881–84, and *Psalm 150* of 1892. With the exception of the *Study Symphony in F Minor* (*Symphony No. 00*) of 1863, and the *Symphony No. 1 in C Minor* of 1866, all of Bruckner's symphonies were written after he moved to Vienna.[6] The enormous effort expended by the composer on the revisions of these massive works is well documented. Five of his nine symphonies (numbers one, two, three, four, and eight) exist in two authentic versions (Schönzeler 1970, 170–72).

From the point-of-view of this study, the Vienna years are somewhat disappointing. Bruckner composed only four short works for winds, but, as would be expected from a composer at the zenith of his creative powers, these are miniature masterpieces of astonishing originality.

DAS HOHE LIED—WAB 74

Bruckner completed this curious work on the last day of December 1876, but revisions of the score occupied him for more than a dozen years. A striking example of evocative tone-painting, the work became problematic since Bruckner's imagination seemingly outpaced all practical considerations. In its original setting *Das hohe Lied* proved to be unperformable, and the composer rescored it several times. The published score is not as Bruckner left it. Hans Wagner, choirmaster of Academic Choral Society of Vienna, arranged it into a usable edition, and his version was published in 1902, eight years after the composer's death (Göllerich/Auer 1974, IV/1: 426–27).

The text is a short, descriptive poem by Heinrich von der Mattig[7]:

Im Tale rauscht die Mühle	In the valley rushes the mill
Und stört des Wand'rers Lied,	And disturbs the wanderer's song,
Bis er durch Waldesdunkel	Until he escapes through the darkness of
Hin auf die Berge flieht.	the forest
	Up to the mountains.

---

[5]Hanslick described the music as "unnatural, bloated, contaminated and decadent" (Schönzeler 1970, 87).

[6]It has long been believed that the *Symphony in D Minor "Die Nullte"* (*Symphony No. 0*) was written in 1863–64 and substantially revised in 1869. Recent research shows that there never was more than one version of this composition, and that it did not exist in any form prior to 1869 (Hawkshaw 1983, 252–63).

[7]Pseudonym for Dr. Heinrich Wallmann, a medical officer in the Austrian Army (Göllerich/Auer 1974, IV/1: 422).

Und immer ferner rauschet	And further and further away rushes
Die Mühle tief im Tal	The mill down in the valley
Und immer kräftiger schallet	And stronger and stronger resounds
Des Liedes Widerhall.	The song's echo.
Die Höhe ist erklommen,	The height is mastered,
Jetzt ist das Lied allein	Now the song is alone
Und schwimmt auf lust'gen Wellen	And is swimming on cheerful waves
Ins Abendrot hinein.	Into the sunset's glow.
(Göllerich/Auer 1974, IV/1: 424)	(Translation by Ruth Thomas)

Bruckner seems to have been fascinated by the Alpine imagery and the symbolism in this poem, and was inspired by the possibilities for tone-painting that it offered him. The original scoring was for three soloists (two tenors and one baritone) and *a capella* male voices divided into two choirs, one of which was a "humming choir" throughout most of the piece. Rehearsals soon revealed that the rather complex parts for the humming choir could not be performed accurately, and Bruckner was advised to double these parts with two violas, two celli, and a double bass. When he undertook this revision, he also added low brass (four horns, three trombones, and tuba), although these parts were never written into the score. A score does exist that includes both the humming choir and the strings, indicating that Bruckner did not want to simply replace the voices with the strings. This new version was rehearsed by the composer himself on December 10, 1879, but was not performed. However, the piece apparently was important to Bruckner, since he returned to it a number of years later (after 1888). He conducted numerous rehearsals, but when it showed only limited improvement after eight or nine attempts, he ceased rehearsing it. In 1895, a year before Bruckner's death, the choir-master, Josef Neubauer, scheduled it for a spring concert, but after two rehearsals it was dropped from the program at the composer's request. Finally, Hans Wagner decided to leave out the enigmatic humming choir altogether. The string parts were retained in place of the humming choir, the soloists were reduced to a single tenor voice, and Bruckner's own brass parts finally were added to the score. Wagner's edition was well received at its first performance on March 13, 1902, and was published shortly afterward (Göllerich/Auer 1974, IV/1: 426–27). Although Wagner included a preface to his edition that explained very carefully how and why he had chosen to adapt the work, this arrangement is hardly an accurate representation of Bruckner's intentions.

Despite its impractically and the problems with its published edition, *Das hohe Lied* is intriguing music. Bruckner structured it in three sections following the versification of Mattig's poem. Since the first two sections are similar, the overall form is a derivation of bar-form. The first six bars of the initial verse are over a tonic pedal (A♭). The humming choir (replaced by low strings in this edition) presents what is, in effect, simultaneous trills or tremolos. This busy, repetitive texture is a graphic depiction of the sound of rushing water and the noise of the mill that is described in the text (Göllerich/Auer 1974, IV/1: 424–25), and is set against the wanderer's song, presented in this version by a solo tenor. The solo line consists of numerous wide skips combined with neighbouring-note figures, and, throughout the verse, is developed sequentially, as was typical of Bruckner's melodic construction at this time.

Example 6.1:
Das hohe Lied—bars 1–6

Much of the harmony of this verse, and of the work as a whole, is third-related and progresses at the rate of one chord/bar. Darkness is portrayed (at the words "he escapes through the darkness of the forest") by a series of diminished-seventh chords, generated by a chromatically descending bass line.

Example 6.2:
Das hohe Lied—bars 11–14 (melody/harmony only)

This sombre sonority is abruptly replaced by "bright" E major at the final line of the stanza "Up to the mountains."

Example 6.3:
Das hohe Lied—bars 15–17

Once arrived, the tonality stabilizes. For five full bars only the tonic and dominant chords of E major are present. The choir, singing mostly in two voices, enters for the first time and supports the soloist in a call-and-response texture. The melody presented by the soloist is repeated by the bass voices of the choir, while the tenors add a "horn fifth" counterpoint, which is apparently intended as another Alpine touch—a hint of distant hunters' horns. A brief, harmonically complex transition using only the humming choir/strings leads to verse two.

The second verse begins exactly like the first, but at a quieter dynamic. Throughout this verse the busy, repetitive texture of the humming choir/strings is gradually simplified, and by the end of the verse has completely faded away. This procedure is an obvious reflection of the words; the sound of the mill gradually fades into the distance as the wanderer ascends the mountain (Göllerich/Auer 1974, IV/1: 425). The choir enters sooner than in the previous verse, supporting the soloist throughout the final two lines of the stanza. This, too, was apparently dictated by the words. Bruckner presumably felt the need for forceful voice parts to enunciate the words "And stronger and stronger resounds the echo's song." Choral textures are similar to those in verse one, but are altered to simulate a precise textual image, the echo. Choir and soloist are still in call-and-response relationship, but the choir echoes the soloist in two different ways.

Example 6.4:
Das hohe Lied—bars 37–41

The "bright" E major that appeared at this point in verse one is replaced by equally brilliant B major in this verse.

Verse three provides a dramatic contrast in both timbre and texture. Both the soloist and the humming choir/strings have disappeared and are replaced by the brass ensemble. The singers are divided into two choirs that respond antiphonally to each other, perhaps another pictorial effect intended to depict the sound of the wanderer's song echoing from the mountaintop. The brass parts simply duplicate the voices; the horns double choir I, while the trombones and tuba double choir II. Overall the texture is simpler, and, as dictated by the text, the first half of this verse is climactic. The harmony consists mostly of major chords, and several spectacular progressions in thirds appear. The final three lines of the poem, starting with the words "And now the song is alone ..." form a musical coda and, as might be expected, are virtually *a capella*. At the beginning of this concluding segment the choirs initiate a very interesting fragmented, imitative texture. Harmonically, these bars turn toward A-flat minor, but appear to be linearly conceived, making precise key identification difficult. For example, in bars 66–68 all of the voices descend chromatically, generating a succession of diminished-seventh chords.

Example 6.5:
Das hohe Lied—bars 66–68

The final image of the poem, the wanderer's joyous song fading into the twilight, instigates a long *diminuendo* (fifteen bars) to the end of the composition. The final chord progression is also prolonged by a gradual slowing of the harmonic rhythm. These four chords, E♭M → C♭M → F♭M → A♭M, form an elongated progression in thirds, but the harmonic context is constantly enriched by moving lines that create many momentary but poignant dissonances.

Example 6.6:
Das hohe Lied—bars 73–75

Considering this closing progression, it cannot be coincidental that F-flat major and C-flat major are the enharmonic equivalents of the only established secondary keys of the two preceding verses. Decorating the final dominant to tonic cadence in this way adds a masterly touch of musical integration, but the progression still sounds rather startling when a conventionally tonal cadence is expected.

Das hohe Lied is an extraordinary work. In its conception it evolved out of the Romantic tradition of descriptive music, but its unique combination of graphic representation of the textual imagery and forward-looking harmony make it unusual music for its time. Also, the harmonized trills and tremolos of the humming choir/strings create a type of "sound cloud," undoubtedly a curious sound to nineteenth-century ears, but a texture that would manifest in numerous ways in the twentieth century.

For conductors, this is a decidedly problematic composition. If performance of any of the original versions (i.e., any version using the humming choir) is contemplated, the conductor is immediately confronted with the same performance obstacles that frustrated Bruckner and his contemporaries in the nineteenth century. The published edition is perhaps the best possible compromise, but it does not really reflect the composer's original intent.

ABENDZAUBER—WAB 57

Another curiosity in Bruckner's *oeuvre*, *Abendzauber* has a number of points-in-common with *Das hohe Lied*. The text is another short poem by Heinrich von der Mattig, and the unusual scoring includes a humming choir. The complete performing forces are: tenor/baritone solo, male chorus (humming choir for much of the piece), four horns, and three yodellers. Bruckner completed this composition on January 13, 1878 (Grasberger 1977, 63), shortly after the disastrous premiere of *Symphony No. 3*. It is one of only three short compositions newly written during all of 1878,[8] and is dedicated to the composer's friend from Steyr, Karl Almeroth.

Despite the performance problems created by the humming choir in *Das hohe Lied*, Bruckner apparently remained intrigued by this novel sound. In this, his second work to incorporate a humming choir, he did, however, simplify the music. Throughout *Abendzauber* the chorus hums long notes or simple moving passages, but the advanced harmonic usage still creates substantial difficulties for the singers.

Mattig's poem is descriptive and atmospheric, and, unlike *Das hohe Lied*, is almost completely devoid of physical action:

Der See träumt zwischen Felsen,
Es flüstert sanft der Hain.
Den Bergeshang beleuchtet
Des Mondes Silberschein.
Und aus dem Waldesdunkel
Hallt Nachtigallensang.
Und von dem See wehn Lieder
Mit zauberhaftem Klang.

Ich saß am Seegestade
Vertieft im süßen Traum;
Da träumte ich zu schweben
Empor zum Himmelsraum ...
Wer könnte je vergessen
Den wonnevollen Ort!
Noch tief im Herzen klingen
Die Zaubertöne fort.

(Göllerich/Auer 1974, IV/1: 490)

The lake is dreaming between the cliffs,
Gently the grove whispers.
The mountain side is lit
By the silvery shine of the moon.
And from the darkness of the forest
Sounds the nightingale's song.
And from the lake songs drift over
With magiclike sound.

I was sitting at the shore of the lake
Absorbed in a sweet dream;
Then I dreamed I was floating
Up to the sphere of Heaven ...
Who could ever forget this blissful place!
Deep in the heart
The magic tones still sound.

(Translation by Ruth Thomas)

---

[8]Bruckner did, however, begin work on the *String Quintet in F* in December of 1878 (Schönzeler 1970, 74).

Like many other Romantics, Bruckner found inspiration and spiritual meaning in the mysteries of the night. Moonlight on a mountain lake provided him with a view into the elemental spirits of nature. The three yodellers in this work were intended to represent these ancient spirits, and, according to Franz Bayer,[9] Bruckner heard them as distant female voices somewhat similar to the Rheinmaidens of Wagner's *Der Ring des Nibelungen*. Because they were mystical creatures, they could sing no identifiable words, and, in fact, Bruckner did not even specify actual syllables, despite considerable urging from Bayer. Viktor Keldorfer, conductor of the Vienna *Männergesang-Verein*, found a workable and appropriate solution by providing the distant voices with the syllables of Alpine yodellers. Keldorfer also furnished optional words for the humming choir, although he carefully maintained Bruckner's original (Göllerich/Auer 1974, IV/1: 490–91, 493), and most performances do not use the words.

Like the poem, Bruckner's music is structured in two verses. However, substantial timbral changes near the end of the second verse, especially the disappearance of the soloist and the conversion of the humming choir to words, give the aural effect of three sections. Since both verses begin with the same music, the overall structure is again reminiscent of bar-form.

The work begins with two bars of quiet horn fanfares that introduce a melodic motive, which is the basis of virtually all melodic material in the piece. Throughout the composition the horn parts consist exclusively of brief fanfares that serve to establish the Alpine atmosphere—they bring to mind the horns of hunters echoing through the mountains—but also have a spiritual function in that they represent the means by which the spirits of nature announce their presence.

Example 6.7:
Abendzauber—bars 1–2

The humming choir appears at bar three. Its G-flat major chord, sustained for four bars, establishes a profound sense of stillness and spaciousness. When the soloist enters at bar four, he outlines an E-flat minor chord against the G-flat major background. However, apart from this brief touch of double-tonic, the opening sixteen bars of the piece are tonally functional within the tonic key—G-flat major. This strict adherence to a "dark" tonality is probably intended as a metaphor for night. As has been noted throughout this study, Bruckner did assign these kinds of programmatic functions to his choices of keys.

---

[9]Bayer was a former pupil who became *regens chori* at the *Stadtpfarrkirche* in Steyr. Under his direction the performance of Bruckner's D Minor Mass became a regular Easter Day event (Schönzeler 1970, 102).

Example 6.8:
Abendzauber—bars 4–6

The key alters at the words "The mountain slope is lit, By the silvery shine of the moon," when the harmony ascends through f minor, G major, and A-flat major to culminate in a very brightly scored E major chord.[10]

The yodellers, presenting the songs of the spirits of nature, first appear, as might be expected, at the words "And from the darkness of the forest..." Musically, they function in antiphonal relationship with the horns and are at first almost imperceptible, which is clearly another poetic device—one must listen carefully to hear the songs of nature. Their music is very similar to that of the horns, consisting of fanfare figures that either outline the primary motive of the work or *arpeggiate* a single chord. Throughout this final segment of verse one, the harmony gradually darkens[11] again, returning to G-flat major through its dominant for the beginning of verse two.

The second verse begins by repeating the initial eleven bars of verse one, with the addition of the yodellers. After these eleven bars the music reaches its major climax quickly. At the words "Up into the sphere of Heaven ...," the soloist and the first tenor voice of the humming choir soar upward over chromatic harmonies to arrive in D major.

Example 6.9:
Abendzauber—bars 51–55

---

[10]The upper voice of the humming choir ascends to G-sharp, and a compound perfect fifth (E → B) appears between the two bass voices.

[11]Göllerich and Auer suggest that this harmonic "darkening" represented clouds blocking the brilliance of the moon (Göllerich/Auer 1974, IV/1: 492).

Again reflecting the sense of the poem, the rest of the work (some twenty-six bars) is at quiet dynamic levels. Bruckner drew attention to this part of his composition by instituting substantial changes of timbre and texture. The soloist disappears, the humming choir is given words for the first time, and the texture, a series of imitative entries, recalls that of *Inveni David*. Like the earlier work, the two middle voices enter together, and the harmony creates a Neapolitan relationship (see Example 4.26).

Example 6.10:
Abendzauber—bars 58–61

Viktor Keldorfer believed that these dramatic changes of the work's soundscape had poetic significance. He suggested that by altering his music so noticeably, Bruckner was intending to draw the listener "from the ethereal heights back to the well grounded earth" (Göllerich/Auer 1974, IV/1: 492–93). This long cadential section is indeed in a more familiar style, and the widely spaced entries of the horns and the yodellers give the music the quality of memory. In the final bars, the tonic (G♭ major) is firmly re-established, but the horn fanfares from the very beginning of the work are repeated, creating an inconclusive finish and providing what is probably yet another metaphor. One almost feels as if the work is starting over again, an effect that is apparently intended as evidence of the eternal character of the spirits of nature.

As in most of the works reviewed in this study, the harmonic structure of *Abendzauber* draws heavily on root progressions of a third. However, this work displays two examples of this process that have not previously appeared. At the beginning of this composition, the harmony functions tonally within the tonic for sixteen bars, although the mediant and sub-mediant of the key are prominently featured. Such harmonic stability within a completely nineteenth-century context has not been observed in earlier compositions in this genre. Also, near the midpoint of verse one, the music modulates around a complete circle of major thirds.

Example 6.11:
Abendzauber—bars 28–33 (harmony only)

While chords related by major thirds are a frequent occurrence in these compositions, circular modulations of this type have not been previously noted.

Abendzauber is another remarkable work, quite unlike anything else in the *oeuvre* of Bruckner or any other composer. While its compositional means are unique, its hushed, other-worldly character was replicated by at least two later composers writing descriptive music on the same subject—Anatole Liadov in *The Enchanted Lake, op. 62* (1909) and Arnold Schönberg in *Summer Morning by the Lake, op. 16, No. 3* (1909). However, Bruckner's composition cannot be considered the prototype for either of these later pieces. Both had already been written by the time the work received its premiere on March 18, 1911 (Grasberger 1977, 63), performed by the Vienna *Männergesang-Verein* under Viktor Keldorfer. It was enthusiastically received by the audience (Göllerich/Auer 1974, IV/1: 493).

Abendzauber is, however, a precursor to another composition by Bruckner. The *Scherzo* of *Symphony No. 6*,[12] and especially its Trio, contains numerous fanfares that recall the figures assigned to both the horns and the yodellers in *Abendzauber* (Göllerich/Auer 1974, IV/1: 491). While it may, in retrospect, be considered a study for the Sixth Symphony, this evocative and atmospheric piece stands alone as a monument to the often surprising imagination of this deeply religious, spiritually inspired composer.

ECCE SACERDOS MAGNUS—WAB 13

This motet, one of Bruckner's crowning achievements in the small forms, was completed on April 20, 1885, and was intended for the celebrations marking the one-hundredth anniversary of the founding of the diocese of Linz.[13] Apparently, it was customary in Linz to feature the works of local composers in major church festivals. Although he was no longer resident in the city in 1885, Bruckner's long association with the cathedral there led to his being invited to submit a new work. He was extremely busy at the time,[14] but obviously wanted to contribute to the festivities (Göllerich/Auer 1974, IV/2: 313). On May 18, 1885, he wrote to Johannes Burgstaller, the choir director of the new cathedral: "Although I had only my hours of relaxation at my disposal for this composition and even these ones not

---

[12]Bruckner composed this movement between December 17, 1880, and January 17, 1881 (Göllerich/Auer 1974, IV/3: 668–69).

[13]An inconsistency around the origin of this work can be observed in some of the Bruckner literature. Certain writers have asserted that it was written to commemorate the one-thousandth anniversary of the diocese of Linz (see, for example, Watson 1977, 104). However, a review of the history of the city reveals that Linz became the See of a bishop in 1785. *Ecce sacerdos magnus*, then, was part of the centennial celebration of the diocese, as noted by Göllerich and Auer, Grasberger, and other scholars.

[14]His major activity at this time was the composition of the *Adagio* of the Eighth Symphony (Göllerich/Auer 1974, IV/3: 672–73).

for very long anymore!!! I still kept my word and am sending you, Reverent sir, the new *Ecce sacerdos magnus*" (Göllerich/Auer 1974, IV/2: 316).

The work gives no indication of having been written quickly. The overall structure is balanced around a plainchant statement of the Lesser Doxology,[15] and the words "*Ideo jurejurando ... suam*," along with the music associated with them, become a type of *ritornello* that provides the work's creative centre. Around this central core Bruckner created a series of contrasting episodes in a variety of textures that seem to trace the evolution of church music from *organum*, through the imitative structures of the Renaissance, to the contrapuntal chorales of the late Baroque. The harmony, however, has little grounding in history. Many chord progressions still sound astonishing more than a century after their creation. Varied textures, bold harmonies, and effective deployment of the performing forces (eight-part chorus, organ, and three trombones) create a commanding work of immense power.

Despite Bruckner's efforts to complete it on time, and the magnificence of the piece itself, *Ecce sacerdos magnus* was not performed in Linz in 1885. Its first performance did not occur until November 21, 1912, when Max Auer and the women's choral society of Vöcklabruck gave the premiere (Göllerich/Auer 1974, IV/2: 315).

As he had so often in the past, Bruckner turned to the Roman Catholic liturgy for his text. His singularly appropriate choice is the Responsory from the ceremony for the Solemn Reception of a Bishop (*Liber Usualis* 1952, 1840–42):

Ecce sacerdos magnus
Qui in diebus suis placuit Deo:

Ideo jurejurando fecit illum Dominus crescere
In plebem suam.

Benedictionem omnium gentium dedit illi,
Et testamentum suum confirmavit super caput ejus.

[Ideo jurejurando ... suam.]

Gloria Patri, et Filio, et Spiritui Sancto.
Sicut erat in principio et nunc,
Et semper, et in saecula saeculorum.
Amen.

Behold a great priest
Who in his days pleased God:

The Lord therefore swore an oath to bless the nations through his descendants.

He granted him the blessing of all peoples,
And confirmed His testament in His own flesh.

[The Lord ... descendants.]

Glory be to the Father, to the Son, and to the Holy Spirit.
As it was in the beginning, is now, and ever shall be.
World without end.
Amen.

---

[15]"Glory be to the Father, and to the Son, and to the Holy Spirit. As it was in the beginning, is now, and ever shall be, world without end. Amen."

[Ideo jurejurando ... suam.]   [The Lord ... descendants.]

(*Liber Usualis* 1952, 1841)   (Proffitt 1991, 13)

Burgstaller had asked Bruckner for a piece that could be performed while the Bishop was entering the church (Göllerich/Auer 1974, IV/2: 313). Bruckner's composition does indeed have the character of a procession, and at the same time it evokes the pageantry and splendour of the entire history of Church ceremony and ritual.

As might be expected considering the words, the work opens forcefully. Choir and trombones present a distinctive rhythmic figure that is based on the speech rhythm of the text and is designed to capture immediately the attention of all listeners. Near derivations of this figure recur in virtually all loud sections of the piece and are an important integrating element.

Example 6.12:
Ecce sacerdos magnus—**bars 1–2 (choir)**

In Bruckner's setting the first verse of the text functions as an introduction to the work as a whole, and its two lines employ texturally and timbrally contrasted music. The initial line comprises two phrases of music, powerfully enunciated by the full ensemble. Harmonically, both phrases begin as open fifths that imply *organum*, and then proceed into triads that do not adhere to any tonality, although this sub-section ends in C major. The second line, which employs only chorus and organ, is set as a five-voice *fugato*. The imitative texture and modal harmony recall the sacred music of the Renaissance. This sub-section also cadences in C major.

The ensuing music (at the words "*Ideo jurejurando ... suam*") is the most striking of the entire composition. As required by the Responsory, it appears three times, creating the *ritornello* around which the piece is constructed. Like the introduction, this music begins forcefully using the full ensemble and incorporating a derivative of the characteristic rhythm. Expanded to eight voices, the singers are separated into female and male choirs responding to each other in antiphonal relationship, like those of the polychoral music of the Renaissance and early Baroque.

The harmony, however, quickly erases any historical associations. The first eight bars of this section present an astonishing chord progression that largely alternates major and minor triads, most of which are related by major thirds. The dramatic effect of these measures is enhanced by the remaining nine bars of the *ritornello*, which are mostly *a capella* and in a simple contrapuntal style.

Example 6.13:
Ecce sacerdos magnus—bars 23–30 (harmony only)

Drama is restored at the "*in plebem suam.*" A sudden, brief annacrusic figure in unison leads to a highly decorated Neapolitan chord on B-flat that resolves to a long cadential passage on its tonic— A major. A rapid *diminuendo* to triple *piano* during these final bars adds to the striking effect of both the climactic Neapolitan chord and its resolution.

Example 6.14:
Ecce sacerdos magnus—bars 33–39

The ensuing words ("*Benedictionem ... ejus*") are a prayer, and, not surprisingly, this section of the music is gentle and intimate. In style, it recalls the contrapuntal chorale settings of J. S. Bach, and much of this music can be analyzed tonally, although it is also marked by the sudden modulations that are typical of Bruckner's writing. The initial line of this verse is repeated, and the two statements form a sequence, despite the fact that the initial chords of the second statement are not an exact transposition. The harmony consists almost exclusively of sixth chords. Consciously or unconsciously, Bruckner incorporated several references to the *Libera me in F Minor* of 1854.

Example 6.15A:
Ecce sacerdos magnus—bars 40–41, 45–47

Example 6.15B:
Libera me—bars 1–2, 20–21

Certain parts of the melodic/harmonic writing are very similar to the earlier composition, as is the use of the augmented sixth chord as a substitute for the dominant.

The remainder of this composition consists of two statements of the *ritornello* separated by the Lesser Doxology. This latter text is enunciated simply in the style of plainsong, using a unison melody that is derived from the Fourth Psalm Tone.

Example 6.16A:
Ecce sacerdos magnus—bars 81–84

Example 6.16B:
Liber Usualis—Fourth Psalm Tone—p. 115

Since the Lesser Doxology is invariably used as the concluding couplet of all the Psalms, Bruckner's association of this plainsong-derived melody with these words is easily understood. However, he also carefully integrated his melody into the composition as a whole. Soprano, alto, and bass lines at the climactic bars of the "*in plebem suam*" (see Example 6.14), and the soprano and tenor melodies at second phrase of the "*Benedictionem ...*" are obviously derived directly from the plainsong. Other melodic fragments are simple transpositions.

Example 6.17:
Ecce sacerdos magnus/Benedictionem ...—bars 41–44

Bruckner probably included the trombones in this score because of their liturgical associations, but they also add substantially to the drama of the music. For the most part, they double the male voices, or whatever three voices are lowest in range at any particular time. However, Bruckner also occasionally extracts lines from the choral textures to create trombone parts that differ from any specific choral line. By doing so, he is able to support all of the voices with only three players. Another clever scoring touch occurs near the end of the *ritornello* (see Example 6.14, bars 4–5). The third of an E major chord is provided by the alto voices only, while the trombones double the rest of the choir.

Ecce sacerdos magnus, a work of almost barbaric intensity, is church music at its most dramatic. In Bruckner's output, it stands stylistically (but not chronologically) between his music for liturgical use, which draws on archaic methods and materials, and the *Te Deum*, with its contemporary harmony and broadly conceived choruses for up to eight voices. Few small-scale works by any composer can match its range of expression, splendour, and dynamic power.

DAS DEUTSCHE LIED—WAB 63

Bruckner completed this short work on April 29, 1892. It was intended for the inaugural German Academic Songfest held in Salzburg, and was first performed in that city on Whitsunday, June 5, 1892, by a massed choir directed by Raoul Mader (Grasberger 1977, 69). Since the work was to be performed by a large male chorus, Bruckner scored the accompaniment for orchestral brass (four horns, three trumpets, three trombones, and tuba), but additional players could also be engaged if necessary. An excellent illustration of this composer's ability to overcome the limitations of a mediocre text, *Das deutsche Lied* is very effective musically.

In 1892 Bruckner was preoccupied with the first movement of the Ninth Symphony, and some of the musical considerations foremost in his mind find expression in this brief choral work. In the harmony, bare, archaic-sounding octaves and open fifths are mixed with lush triadic sonorities and some startlingly dissonant chords. Although the work begins in what appears to be D minor, ends in D major, and contains a few short passages of functional harmony, most of it cannot be analyzed within any key. Pedal tones and unison passages establish whatever sense of tonic can be heard, but the harmony is dominated by stepwise root progressions that project little feeling of tonality. Since this piece is scored for brass instruments, much of the melodic construction is similar to the brass writing found in Bruckner's late symphonies. The style is declamatory, employing fanfare figures that either forcefully reiterate a single pitch or outline *arpeggios*. Double-dotted and triplet rhythms predominate.

The text, a short poem by Erich Fels,[16] was suggested to Bruckner by Dr. Wähner, head of the Academic Choral Society in Vienna (Göllerich/Auer 1974,

---

[16]Pseudonym of Prof. Aurelius Polzer, a teacher at the *Hochschule* in Graz (Grasberger 1977, 69).

IV/3: 235). Like countless other nineteenth-century German poems, it is a fiercely patriotic (even jingoistic) call to German nationalism:

Wie durch's Bergtal dumpf grollt Donnergedröh'n,	As through the mountain valley the thunder muted rolls,
Wie der Sturmwind saust um waldige Höh'n,	As round the wooded height the storm wind howls,
Wie die Meerflut tost an klippigem Strand,	As onto the rocky shore the sea-tide roars,
So schalle, so schmettere, die Feinde zu schrecken,	Let the German Song resound, ring out! Frightening foes and awakening our
Die schlafferen Brüder vom Schlafe zu wecken,	brothers from sleep,
Der deutsche Gesang durch's gefährdete Land!	The German Song resounds, Rings out through our imperiled Land!

(Proffitt 1991, 14)

(Göllerich/Auer 1974, IV/3: 235)

As has been previously noted in this study, the texts of most of his secular works seem to have meant little to Bruckner. In this case, he fortunately did not permit these uninspired words to negatively affect his music, although the militaristic imagery of the poem undoubtedly influenced his choice of marching rhythms and "military" instruments.

Structurally, *Das deutsche Lied* conforms to no identifiable formal pattern, but evolves effortlessly out of the first choral statement. A silent *fermata* at bar 54, followed by a slower tempo, separates the final line of text from the rest of the composition. Musically, these final bars, approximately one-third of the total work, are the climax of the piece and function as a coda.

The work opens with a four bar fanfare consisting of several octaves of the single pitch D, which immediately identifies its composer.[17]

Example 6.18:
Das deutsche Lied—bars 1–5

Some writers have connected this passage, with its double- and triple-dotted

---

[17]If this fanfare is not enough, his identity is revealed a few measures later. At bars 14–15, a harmonic descent of a major third, from E-flat major to C-flat major, quickly removes all doubt as to the authorship of this music.

rhythms, to the sketches for the incomplete Finale of the Ninth Symphony,[18] a contention that seems difficult to support since Bruckner did not begin work on those sketches until 1894 (Watson 1977, 151). This passage is, however, similar to the brass fanfares that conclude the first movement of *Symphony No. 9*—music with which the composer was actively involved in the spring of 1892. It is also clearly related to the "Death Announcement" motive from the first movement of *Symphony No. 8*.[19]

Example 6.19:
Symphony No. 8—Mvt. 1—bars 255–61

The rhythm introduced in these opening bars is very important. Virtually all of the melodic material in the work incorporates double- or triple-dotted figures, and the primary unifying element throughout the composition is the consistency of rhythm from motive to motive.

Harmonically, the work provides a number of delightful surprises. The first occurs at bar seven, near the end of the initial choral entry. This passage begins in unison, hints at D minor, then moves through a couple of open fifths, and climaxes on a startling chord that initially appears to be a triad on D with simultaneous perfect and diminished fifths.

Example 6.20:
Das deutsche Lied—bars 5–8

---

[18]See Proffitt 1991, 8.

[19]Ascribing programmatic meanings to passages in Bruckner's symphonies is a tricky business. He, himself, did so only when pressured by his friends who felt that such extra-musical devices would help his symphonies be accepted by a wider audience. He revealed his personal feelings on the matter when Joseph Schalk provided a pictorial guide to the Seventh Symphony for a Vienna performance. Bruckner angrily retorted, "If he must write poetry, why should he pick on my symphony?" (Watson 1977, 77).

This particular motive from *Symphony No. 8* presents a rather different case. The designation "annunciation of Death" was assigned to it by Bruckner himself, in a letter to the conductor Felix Weingartner, dated January 27, 1891 (Redlich 1955, 99–100).

However, the subsequent chord is an incomplete triad on A, which implies that the progression in bar seven and eight is intended to be understood as vii°⁷ → I (or i) in A, with the root of the tonic appearing early and serving as the bass of both chords.

A similar analysis can be undertaken to explain a complex harmonic issue that arises near the end of the work.

Example 6.21:
Das deutsche Lied—bars 77–81

At first glance the harmony of these bars is perplexing indeed. The sonority in bar 77 appears to be a chord cluster F♯ → B, that of bar 78 is apparently a dominant ninth on A, bar 79 seems to present a chord in fifths based on G, and bars 80–81 display a conventional V⁷ → I cadence in the final tonic of this piece—D major. The obvious difficulties with this analysis can be eliminated by identifying the pedal A throughout these bars as the root of the dominant seventh chord, which has arrived three bars early. With this assumption, these harmonies can be analyzed as functioning tonally within D major: the chord in bar 77 is seen to be a subdominant major seventh, while those in bars 78–79 are the supertonic and supertonic seventh, respectively. Overall, then, these bars conform to a rather conventional cadential formula.

Although these examples can be understood in terms of customary tonal practice, their effect is anything but orthodox. In both cases, Bruckner's voicing of the chords is designed to emphasize the dissonance, and what the listener hears is several remarkably fresh, and captivating sonorities that clearly have their origin in the Ninth Symphony.

This work also contains two extensive passages that consist exclusively of unresolved seventh chords. Perhaps the most dramatic of the two occurs at bars 51–54, immediately preceding the *fermata* that identifies the beginning of the coda.[20] Throughout these bars Bruckner presents a series of mostly dominant seventh sonorities built on roots that rise chromatically from G to B. The accompanying trumpet fanfares and the silence that follows the final dominant seventh (on B) add substantially to the tension generated by this passage. The ensuing chord, E-flat major, is totally unexpected, although it is worth noting that these two chords (B major and E-flat major) are a major third apart. Progressions and keys related by major thirds have been observed in virtually all of the works in Bruckner's mature

---

[20]The other passage occurs at bars 29–36.

style that have been reviewed in this study.

Example 6.22:
Das deutsche Lied—bars 50–55

A few years later, in the *Adagio* of the Ninth Symphony, Bruckner was to return to this idea and develop it contrapuntally to generate even more tension.

Example 6.23:
Symphony No. 9—Adagio—bars 148–50

In 1882, ten years before the composition of *Das deutsche Lied*, Bruckner was engaged to write a work for the *Oberösterreichisches-Salzburgisches Sängerbundesfest*.[21] The composition he produced, *Sängerbund*, contained a quotation from Johann Wenzel Kalliwoda's much-performed male chorus *Das deutsche Lied*.[22] A decade later, when he was composing a work using the same title as Kalliwoda's popular piece, Bruckner apparently could not resist incorporating another quotation. The borrowed passage appears in the coda, and Bruckner took considerable pains to ensure that it would be recognizable. These seven bars are presented by the choir alone, and consist of a unison descending fragment of a D major scale followed by an unadorned authentic cadence in the tonic.

---

[21] *Germanenzug* was written for this same festival some seventeen years earlier. It was performed at the festival, which was held in Linz, on June 5, 1865.

[22] Kalliwoda was born in 1801 and died in 1866. He was most productive compositionally during the years 1825–1850. His chorus, *Das deutsche Lied*, achieved astonishing popularity and longevity, appearing regularly on the programs of German choirs for nearly a century —well into the 1930s (Sadie 1980, IX: 779–80).

Example 6.24:
Das deutsche Lied—bars 62–69

Within the surrounding context, the simplicity of these bars is striking, and their intent would probably have been immediately obvious to the singers and to their audience. However, as has been observed in other works, whenever Bruckner employed a reference to an external source he carefully integrated it into the work as a whole. Hints of Kalliwoda's phrase appear throughout the coda, although Bruckner's own harmonic usage is never so simple as that displayed in the quotation.[23]

Das deutsche Lied is a miniature masterpiece—an excellent example of a major composer expressing himself very effectively in a small-scale setting. At its premiere in Salzburg, it was received with much enthusiasm, which must have pleased the composer. Bruckner apparently thought well of it. He called it a "*Kracher*" (Göllerich/Auer 1974, IV/3: 236), an untranslatable term, something akin to the North American expression "a barn-burner." One can easily imagine that the cheerful, uncomplicated, and life-affirming character of this piece provided him with an enjoyable respite from his struggles with the monumental, death-haunted music of the Ninth Symphony.

Das deutsche Lied was Bruckner's last composition for winds (he was to produce only a handful of works in any genre in the ensuing four years before his death), and, as such, occupies a significant place in the repertoire. It also presents some of his best music. Along with the other works reviewed in this chapter, it provides the wind ensemble with a fascinating glimpse into the mature style of one of the great harmonic innovators of the nineteenth century.

---

[23]A good example of this occurs during the next choral entry (bars 71–74) following the quotation. Kalliwoda's melody appears in the bass, but the harmony is not so straightforward.

Chapter 7

Striding into Eternity

The final years of Bruckner's life were marked by frequent illness, by the titanic struggle to complete the Finale of the Ninth Symphony, and by growing international recognition. His battles with physical illness began a decade earlier. In 1885 he began to be affected by a form of dropsy, and water retention in his legs and feet—symptoms we now recognize as the onset of heart disease (Schönzeler 1970, 87). By the early 1890s he had developed chronic catarrh (inflammation) of the throat. The combination of problems kept him bedridden for much of 1893 (Watson 1977, 149–50). By early 1895 he was having difficulty climbing the steps to his fourth-floor apartment at Hessgasse 7, and the Emperor put at his disposal the *Kustodenstöckl*, the gate-keeper's lodge at the Belvedere Palace. Bruckner and his housekeeper moved in July 1895, and he was to reside there until his death. The last photograph of Bruckner, taken on July 17, 1896, shows the frail composer, obviously ill, standing in the doorway of the *Kustodenstöckl* in the company of his housekeeper, his brother Ignaz, and his doctor (Schönzeler 1970, 103–6). In the final weeks of his life, he was able to work for only short periods of time, and his associates reported depression and hints of religious mania (Redlich 1955, 25).

Throughout his struggles with ill health, he remained determined to complete the Finale of the Ninth Symphony. This was to have been his most monumental symphonic creation, conceived on an enormous scale, and dedicated "to the King of Kings, our Lord." Bruckner began working on it in November 1894, and fervently declared, "I hope [God] will grant me enough time to complete it." It preoccupied him for the next two years (Watson 1977, 48). Today, the extensive sketches (some 200 pages) fill a complete volume of the *Collected Works*, but the movement remains unfinished.

During these final years Bruckner also achieved international stature. His seventieth birthday (September 4, 1894) was spent in relative seclusion at Steyr, but was celebrated all over the world. He received dozens of congratulatory tele-

grams and many organizations conferred honourary memberships upon him (Schönzeler 1970, 102, 106). The Seventh Symphony, composed between 1881 and
1883 (Göllerich/Auer 1974, IV/3: 670), quickly entered the orchestral repertory,
and other works, notably the *Te Deum* (with some 30 performances during the
composer's lifetime), also began to be heard on a regular basis (Schönzeler 1970,
127, 130). Even in Vienna, where the musical establishment had always been
hostile, his compositions began to receive acceptance. An 1893 performance of the
F-minor Mass was warmly applauded, and the *Te Deum*, performed on January 12,
1896, was also well received (Watson 1977, 47–48).[1] It seems profoundly regret-
table that such acclaim should have come to him at a time when declining health
prevented him from enjoying it.

On Sunday, October 11, 1896, Anton Bruckner worked during the morning on
the last movement of the Ninth Symphony. In the early afternoon he walked in the
beautiful gardens of the Belvedere Palace, and very quietly died in his sleep later
that afternoon (Watson 1977, 48).

His funeral was held three days later, on October 14, 1896, in Vienna's great
Baroque church, the *Karlskirche* (Redlich 1955, 25). The church was packed to
capacity, and several of the city's most important performing groups participated
in the ceremony. The *Männergesang-Verein* performed Herbeck's *Libera* for voices
and wind instruments, and the choir of the *Gesellschaft der Musikfreunde* under
Richard von Perger sang Schubert's *Am Tage Allerseelen* ("Anton Bruckner" 896,
4). Two of the composer's most important contemporaries, Hugo Wolf and
Johannes Brahms, were not present.[2] Wolf was turned away at the door because he

---

[1] The performance of the *Te Deum* was the last concert attended by the composer. He was
so ill that he had to be carried to and from the theatre (Watson 1977, 48).

[2] Hugo Wolf was a student at the Vienna Conservatory during the 1870s when Bruckner
was teaching there, but the two men apparently never met (Redlich 1955, 114). Bruckner
finally made Wolf's acquaintance in 1884, and the latter immediately became an ardent
promoter of his music (Watson 1977, 40). Wolf wrote extensively in the popular press, and
his vitriolic attacks on the Viennese musical establishment may well have contributed to the
hostility with which Bruckner's works were received in the Imperial Capital. The two men
remained friends throughout Bruckner's life. In January 1894, during a rare improvement in
Bruckner's health, they travelled together to Berlin to hear performances of Bruckner's *Te
Deum* and *Symphony No. 7* and Wolf's *Der Feuerreiter* and *Elfenlied* (Schönzeler 1970,
102). Wolf was one of the last people to visit Bruckner before his death (Redlich 1955, 25).

The relationship between Bruckner and Brahms was ambivalent to say the least. Since
Brahms was the darling of the Viennese musical establishment, he and Bruckner were often
cast as opponents in the popular press. Their personal relationship seems always to have
been cordial, although both of them on occasion aimed barbed comments at each other's
work. Brahms is reported to have called Bruckner's symphonies "symphonic boaconstrictors"
and a "swindle that will be forgotten in a few years." For his part, Bruckner apparently
claimed that he preferred a Johann Strauss waltz to a Brahms symphony (Watson 1977, 45,
57–59). Brahms seems to have felt differently about Bruckner's choral music. He applauded

(continued...)

was not a member of one of the "official" music associations, and Brahms, who was seriously ill, declined the offer of admission[3] (Schönzeler 1970, 108). After the service, Bruckner's body was transported to St. Florian, where it was interred under the organ.

"Bruckner, who had entered Vienna as a poor music teacher, left the capital like a prince and went home, to his beloved St. Florian" (Doernberg 1960, 110). He is reported to have remarked that when God called on him to account for his earthly accomplishments, "I will present to Him the score of my *Te Deum*, and He will judge me mercifully" (Watson 1977, 49).

From the perspective of wind research, Bruckner's funeral holds two points of interest. As discussed in chapter 4, the composer requested that the second movement of *Germanenzug* ("*In Odin's Hallen ...*") be performed at his funeral. This request was fulfilled by the Academic Choral Society and a horn quartet from the Court Opera conducted by Dr. Josef Neubauer, while the coffin was being carried out of the Belvedere Palace and placed on the hearse for transport to the *Karlskirche* ("Anton Bruckner" 1896, 4). The service in the church was concluded by a performance of part of the *Adagio* of the Seventh Symphony in an arrangement for wind instruments by Ferdinand Löwe—a work that to date has received only a passing mention in the literature.

ADAGIO FROM *SYMPHONY NO. 7*

The Seventh Symphony took two years to compose, from September 1881 to September 1883. Its premiere performance, which was enthusiastically received, was conducted by Arthur Nikisch in Leipzig on December 30, 1884 (Göllerich/-Auer 1974, IV/3: 670). The work quickly established itself in the international orchestral repertory, and, even today, remains one of Bruckner's most-performed compositions.

The *Adagio* was written during the spring of 1883. Bruckner began working on it on January 22, 1883, and had it completed by April 21 (Göllerich/Auer 1974, IV/3: 670). The mournful primary theme, scored for Wagner tubas, apparently was

---

[2](...continued)

the *F-minor Mass* so enthusiastically in November 1893 that Bruckner personally thanked him. Also, when Richard von Perger became conductor of the choir of the *Gesellschaft der Musikfreunde* in 1895, Brahms, whose opinion carried immense weight in Vienna, advised him to program a Bruckner choral work as soon as possible. Perger complied by performing the *Te Deum* on January 12, 1896—the last time Bruckner was to hear any of his own music. Bruckner had his own poetic summation of their relationship: "He is Brahms—my profound respect. But I am Bruckner, and I prefer my own stuff" (Doernberg, 1960, 89).

[3]Interestingly, the writer of Bruckner's obituary in the *Deutsche Zeitung* identified Brahms as one of the "gentlemen" who gathered at the church prior to the funeral service ("Anton Bruckner" 1896, 4). All scholars concur, however, that Brahms was not present for the service itself.

inspired by a premonition that Wagner's death was imminent. In a letter to Felix Mottl, the composer wrote: "One day I came home and felt very sad. The thought had crossed my mind that before long the Master would die, and then the C-sharp minor theme of the *Adagio* came to me" [4] (Schönzeler 1970, 80).

Bruckner's omen proved accurate. He had reached the great C major climax (with its much-debated cymbal crash)[5] in the recapitulation of this movement (bar 177 of the orchestral score) when the news from Venice reached him that Wagner had died suddenly on February 13. Since Bruckner had always venerated Wagner as something akin to a God, the death of his mentor affected him deeply. The *Adagio* was extended by a substantial and profoundly sad coda, again featuring Wagner tubas, that Bruckner always referred to as "funeral music for the Master" (Schönzeler 1970, 80).

Considering Wagner's overwhelming influence on Bruckner's life, the elegy composed for Wagner was an appropriate choice for the conclusion of his own funeral. Löwe chose to transcribe only the recapitulation of the movement, and scored his arrangement for a large brass ensemble consisting of four trumpets, four horns, four Wagner tubas, three trombones, tuba, and percussion (timpani, tam-tam, and snare drum).[6] Almost none of the "busy" string figuration, which in the original score distinguishes this section from the exposition, appears in the brass arrangement, undoubtedly because it was not idiomatic to these instruments. Löwe also

---

[4]It cannot be coincidental, therefore, that in this particular movement Bruckner employs Wagner tubas for the first time.

[5]The holograph score shows that the percussion parts at this point (timpani, triangle, and cymbals) were added to the music after the movement was finished. Later, they were crossed out and the direction *gilt nicht* (invalid) was written on the score. Researchers have been unable to determine whether this direction is in Bruckner's hand (Simpson 1967, 151). It is clear, however, that the percussion parts were not the composer's idea. A letter from Joseph Schalk to his brother Franz, dated January 10, 1885, indicates that Bruckner was persuaded to add the parts by the Schalk brothers and Arthur Nikisch: "Nikisch has insisted on the acceptance of our desired cymbal crash in the *Adagio*, as also on triangle and timpani, which pleases us immensely" (Watson 1977, 119–20).

Retention of these parts is really a matter of personal preference, since the climax is equally effective with or without them.

These climactic bars employ a sequential presentation of the theme Bruckner used in his *Te Deum* at the words "*Non confundar in aeternum*" ("let me never be misunderstood"). Since the first version of the *Te Deum* preceded the Seventh Symphony, it seems likely that the use of this theme had extra-musical meaning (Schönzeler 1970, 80). Bruckner intended it as a fervent plea for greater understanding of Wagner's—and, by extension, his own— music.

[6]The autograph score of Löwe's arrangement is preserved, on microfilm, in the music collection of the Österreichischen Nationalbibliothek, Wien, under the call number PhA 1529. I am indebted to the Internationale Bruckner-Gesellschaft and Dr. Andrea Harrandt for their assistance in locating this manuscript.

excised measures 193 to 206 of the orchestral version, which were originally scored very transparently for strings and solo woodwinds, and comprise a simplified reference to the closing element of the primary thematic group. Perhaps he felt that these bars would not sound well on brass instruments, or that they were inappropriate musically, considering that his arrangement would include only the final part of the movement. In place of these measures, he provided two alternative endings. The first, composed by Löwe himself, brings the music to a quick conclusion in the minor mode. It was this ending that was performed at Bruckner's funeral ("Anton Bruckner" 1896, 4). The second is Bruckner's own extended, quiet ending (bars 207–19 of the orchestral score), featuring the horns playing a transfigured version of the primary theme. Like the original, it ends in the major mode, but is enharmonically changed from C-sharp to D-flat major. At Bruckner's funeral in the *Karlskirche*, Löwe's arrangement was performed by the brass players of the *Hofopernorchester* under their principal conductor, Hans Richter ("Anton Bruckner" 1896, 4).

Löwe adhered to the original by maintaining the fundamental key (C-sharp minor), and by carefully preserving the soloistic role of the Wagner tubas. However, beyond this, he scored his arrangement to take advantage of the timbral possibilities of the brass ensemble. The parts for the horns, Wagner tubas, and trombones are not necessarily as they were in the original. In order to duplicate the rhythmic energy generated by the string figuration in the orchestral score, Löwe added numerous short fanfares that increase in frequency as the music approaches the grand C major climax. The controversial cymbal crash at this point is replaced by *tam-tam*, which was undoubtedly very impressive in the confines of the church. Trumpet, horn, and Wagner tuba parts are written without key signatures, and many of the pitches are changed enharmonically to simplify reading.

Several other alterations are difficult to justify. Löwe shortened the climax by one bar and ended it with a *fermata* that is silent except for a quiet snare drum roll (which certainly should be muted in performance). There seems to be no logical reason for truncating the climax, and, while the *fermata* and snare drum roll are admittedly effective, they represent a substantial recomposition of the original—a liberty that seems unnecessary considering the quality of Bruckner's music.

Löwe's wind instrument transcription presents a portion of this beautiful movement, and is not, as is stated in much of the literature, "an arrangement of the *Adagio* of the Seventh Symphony." It was obviously intended specifically for the members of the *Hofopernorchester*, who had easy access to and experience with Wagner tubas, and provided them and their conductor with the opportunity to participate in Bruckner's funeral. On the other hand, it was a singularly apt farewell to this great composer, and apparently had a profound impact[7] on all of those pre-

---

[7]For confirmation see the introduction to the score of the *Symphony No. 7* in the Vienna Philharmonic edition, published by Universal Edition (no date given). This introduction was written by Josef V. Wöss, who was present at Bruckner's funeral.

sent. There can be no question that this music is effectively scored for its new medium, and may still provide contemporary wind ensembles with a vehicle for directly experiencing at least part of one of Bruckner's most exquisite creations.

The works reviewed in this study represent a substantial and important contribution to the wind repertoire specifically, and to the musical literature in general. Certain of these compositions, particularly the *E-minor Mass* and the sacred motets with trombones, have established themselves as works of substance and receive many performances. However, several other pieces, notably, *Psalm 114; Cantata: Auf, Brüder! auf, und die Saiten zur Hand!; Festcantata: Preiset den Herrn; Germanenzug; Marsch in Es-Dur; Abendzauber;* and *Das deutsche Lied*, are works of genius that deserve a much more prominent place in the consciousness of music lovers.

Bruckner composed wind music at every stage in his career. Many of these works represented a marked development in his musical accomplishment (*Psalm 114, Libera me, Vor Arneths Grab, Germanenzug,* etc.) and pointed to the direction his creative thinking would take. They form an integral link in the continuous evolution of his compositional maturation, and are essential to any understanding of his ultimate achievement.

And what an achievement it was! As Schönzeler asserts,

Bruckner's musical roots reach back to Palestrina, to Bach, to Beethoven and Schubert, and his formal outlook is fashioned by the baroque of St. Florian and by the gothic of the *Stadtpfarrkirche* in Steyr and later of the *Stephansdom* in Vienna. His music contains passages of the deepest mysticism ... [and] melodies which take us back to the folksong and folk dances of Upper Austria ... In every bar of his music he strives towards his "dear Lord", searches for him in the expanse of the universe and in the narrow confines of his native countryside. ... it has been said that each of his symphonies is in reality one gigantic arch which starts on earth in the midst of suffering humanity, sweeps up toward the heavens to the very Throne of Grace, and returns to earth with a message of peace (Schönzeler 1970, 169).

From the perspective of a century and with the knowledge of the magnitude of his accomplishments, we now understand that the withering criticism inflicted on this great composer during his lifetime was unjustified and myopic. Today, we can easily visualize Bruckner's critics trapped within the narrow confines of their own limited view of the world, while he, with giant steps, strides over them into eternity.

Appendix A: The *Apollo-Marsch*—WAB 115

The authorship of the *Apollo-Marsch* has long been subject to question. It seems to have first been attributed to Bruckner in 1897 by Heinrich Rietsch (Hawkshaw 1989, 8), and this contention was supported by Max Graf in 1902. Graf claimed, without providing any documentation, that both this march and the *March in E-Flat Major* were composed for the band of the *Jäger* battalion in Linz in 1865 (Graf 1902, 584). However, since this march exists only in a handwritten, fair-copy manuscript that is unattributed and undated, Bruckner scholars had begun to question this attribution by the 1930s. It was generally surmised that the *Apollo-Marsch* became associated with Bruckner because the score was among his papers at the time of his death. Unfortunately, very poor records were kept of the distribution of the composer's effects, and it is no longer possible to confirm whether he ever owned this manuscript (Hawkshaw 1989, 10).

The widely accepted view is that the score of the *Apollo-Marsch* was given to Bruckner during the summer of 1865 to serve as a model for his *E-Flat Major March*. The two works do have a number of similarities. Both are in the same key, both are scored for identical ensembles, and both use approximately the same form. However, Bruckner studied the march form with Otto Kitzler early in 1862 (Hawkshaw 1989, 10), and it is possible that this score was given to him at that time if, indeed, he ever owned it at all.

In 1984 Werner Probst proved that the *Apollo-Marsch* is identical to the *Mazzuchelli March, op. 22* by the Hungarian composer, violinist, and bandmaster Kéler Béla (Probst 1984, 6). Kéler was the bandmaster of the 10th Austrian Infantry Regiment in Vienna in 1856 (Suppan 1988, 193–94). He wrote this march in 1857, dedicating it to the *Feldzeugmeister* Alois Count Mazzuchelli (Probst 1984, 6). It would appear, then, that the only question left unresolved is how this work managed to change titles between 1857 and either 1862 or 1865.

In retrospect, how the *Apollo-Marsch* could ever have been attributed to Bruckner is difficult to understand. Other than its superficial similarities to the *March in E-Flat*, this work bears not the slightest resemblance to Bruckner's style. The harmonic usage is rudimentary, rarely employing more than the most common chords within the key, the full ensemble is deployed almost constantly, and the second strain is based on a simplistic, rather clichéd melody. While this is certainly pleasant, tuneful music, it is a straightforward, functional composition that makes no attempt to stretch the boundaries of the form. Bruckner would never have placed such limitations on his creativity.

Appendix B: *Litanei—WAB 132*

Bruckner frequently made reference to a *Litanei* for mixed choir and brass instruments that he supposedly composed in 1844. It retained a special place in his consciousness because Sechter had praised it (Göllerich/Auer 1974, I: 253). A letter from Sechter indicates that Bruckner had sent him the score of this work and requested his evaluation. Sechter apparently liked it since he remarked that he was pleased it had been positively received. The *Litanei* must have been performed in Linz sometime shortly after Bruckner moved there in 1856, but no trace of the score can be found today (Göllerich/Auer 1974, III/1: 55–56).

Appendix C: Sources

Bruckner's popular works for winds, the *E-minor Mass* and the motets with trombones, are available in many editions. Most of the lesser-known pieces are not published in commercial performing sets, but reference scores appear in the *Collected Works* or in Göllerich and Auer. This list identifies locations where these scores can be found, including commercial publications, where they exist. Some of the secular works have not yet been published in the *Collected Works* and do not appear in Göllerich and Auer. These compositions exist in old, but still available, commercial printings, which are also identified. For information regarding manuscripts, see Göllerich/Auer 1974, II/1: 366–79; III/1: 643–63; IV/3: 658–77.

Choralmesse in C-Dur (Windhaager)—WAB 25: Collected Works, Band 21, No. 2, 4–11; Göllerich/Auer, I: 173–89; Carus-Verlag, No. 40.759/01.

Missa ex G-moll pro Quadragesima—WAB 140: Collected Works, Band 21, No. 42, 172; Göllerich/Auer, II/2: 84–85.

Zwei Aequale—WAB 114, 149: Collected Works, Band 21, No. 14, 52–53; Göllerich/Auer, II/2: 83 (1st *Aequali* only).

Psalm 114—WAB 36: Collected Works, Band 20, No. 1, 1–20; Göllerich/Auer, II/2: 152–77 (facsimile).

Cantata: Heil, Vater! Dir zum hohen Feste—WAB 61: Collected Works, Band 22, Teil 1, No. 3a, 57–75; (This work does appear in Göllerich/Auer, II/2: 131–40, but is incomplete, and the text is a mixture of this first version and that of the second version from 1857).

Libera me—WAB 22: Collected Works, Band 21, No. 17, 58–67; Doblinger, No. 45 304.

Vor Arneths Grab—WAB 53: Göllerich/Auer, II/2: 184–88.

Laßt Jubeltöne laut erklingen—WAB 76: Göllerich/Auer, III/2: 161–179.

Cantata: Auf, Brüder! auf, und die Saiten zur Hand!—WAB 60: Collected Works, Band 22, Teil 1, No. 4, 97–126; Göllerich/Auer, II/2: 229–39.

Cantata: Auf, Brüder! auf zur frohen Feier!—WAB 61: Collected Works, Band 22, Teil 1, No 3b, 77–95; (This work does appear in Göllerich/Auer, II/2: 131–40, but is incomplete, and the text is a mixture of the first version from 1852 and this second version from 1857).

Afferentur regi—WAB 1: Collected Works, Band 21, No. 21, 86–87; many commercial editions.

Festcantata: Preiset den Herrn—WAB 16: Collected Works, Band 22. Teil 2, No. 6, 147–77; Göllerich/Auer, III/2: 197–216 (facsimile).

Germanenzug—WAB 70: Collected Works, Band 22, Teil 2, 179–212.

Marsch in Es-Dur—WAB 116: Collected Works, Band 12/8, 1–12 (this edition includes parts); Göllerich/Auer, III/2: 225–33 (facsimile).

Inveni David—WAB 19: Collected Works, Band 21, No. 23, 90–93; Göllerich/-Auer, III/2: 239–44 (facsimile); many commercial editions.

E-minor Mass—WAB 27: Collected Works, Band 17/1 (1866 version); and 17/2 (1882 version); many commercial editions.

Das hohe Lied—WAB 74: Doblinger, No. 2693 (1902), (University of Iowa, Music, M1538, B9 H6).

Abendzauber—WAB 57: Universal Edition, No. 2914 (1911).

Ecce sacerdos magnus—WAB 13: Collected Works, Band 21, No. 33, 130–40; many commercial editions.

Das deutsche Lied—WAB 63: Universal Edition, No. 3300 (1911).

Adagio from *Symphony No. 7*: Arranged for brass instruments by F. Löwe, Musiksammlung, Österreichischen Nationalbibliothek, Wien, Call No. PhA 1529 (autograph manuscript).

Apollo-Marsch: Collected Works, Band 12/8 Anhang, 13–28.

Bibliography

"Anton Bruckner" in *Deutsche Zeitung*, Wien, October 15, 1896, 4.

Apel, Willi, ed. (1972) *Harvard Dictionary of Music*. 2nd. ed., Cambridge, Mass: The Belknap Press of Harvard University Press.

Bailey, Robert. (1985) "An Analytical Study of the Sketches and Drafts" in *Richard Wagner: Prelude and Transfiguration from Tristan and Isolde*. Ed. by Robert Bailey. New York: W. W. Norton & Co., 113–46.

Bauernfeind, Hans, and Leopold Nowak, eds. (1984) *Anton Bruckner: Samtliche Werke. Vol. XXI—Kleine Kirchenmusikwerke*. Wien: Musikwissenschaftlicher Verlag der Internationalen Bruckner-Gesellschaft.

Bornhöft, Rüdiger, ed. (1996) *Anton Bruckner: Samtliche Werke. Vol. XII, Part 8—Marsch in Es-Dur and Anhang: Apollo-Marsch*. Wien: Musikwissenschaftlicher Verlag der Internationalen Bruckner-Gesellschaft.

Burkhart, Franz, Rudolf H. Führer, and Leopold Nowak, eds. (1987) *Anton Bruckner: Samtliche Werke. Vol. XXII, Part 1–2—Kantaten und Chorwerke*. Wien: Musikwissenschaftlicher Verlag der Internationalen Bruckner-Gesellschaft.

Cooke, Deryck, and Leopold Nowak. (1980) "Bruckner (Joseph) Anton" in *The New Grove Dictionary of Music and Musicians*. 20 vols. ed. by Stanley Sadie. London: Macmillan, vol. III, 352–71.

Cooke, Deryck, and Leopold Nowak. (1985) "Anton Bruckner" in *The New Grove Late Romantic Masters*. New York: W. W. Norton & Co., 1–73.

Doernberg, Erwin. (1960) *The Life and Symphonies of Anton Bruckner*. London: Barrie and Rockliff.

Göllerich, August, and Max Auer. (1974) *Anton Bruckner. Ein Lebens- und Scaffensbild*. 9 vols. Regensburg: Gustav Bosse Verlag.

Graf, Max. (1902) "Anton Bruckner II: Der Entwickelungsgang" in *Die Musik*, I (Zweites Quartal, 1901–2), 580–85.

Grasberger, Renate. (1977) *Werkverzeichnis Anton Bruckner*. Tutzing: Verlegt bei Hans Schneider.

Gruber, Gerold Wolfgang. (1988) "Die Credo-Kompositionen Anton Bruckners" in *Bruckner Symposion: Anton Bruckner und die Kirchenmusik*. Linz: Anton Bruckner Institut, 129–43.

Hamilton, Edith. (1963) *Mythology*. Toronto: Mentor Books.

Hawkshaw, Paul. (1983) "The Date of Bruckner's 'Nullified' Symphony in D Minor" in *19th Century Music*, Vol. VI, No. 3 (Spring 1983), 252–63.

Hawkshaw, Paul. (1984) *The Manuscript Sources for Anton Bruckner's Linz Works: A Study of His Working Methods from 1856 to 1868*. Ann Arbor, MI: University Microfilms International (8505979).

Hawkshaw, Paul. (1989) "Anton Bruckner and the *Apollo March* for Band" in *College Band Directors National Association Journal*, VI, (Autumn 1988/Winter 1989), 8–10.

Hawkshaw, Paul. (1990) "From Zigeunerwald to Valhalla in Common Time: The Genesis of Anton Bruckner's *Germanenzug*" in *Bruckner Jahrbuch 1987/88*. Linz: Anton Bruckner Institut Linz: Linzer Veranstaltungsgesellschaft mbH, 21–30.

Hawkshaw, Paul, ed. (1997) *Anton Bruckner: Samtliche Werke. Vol. XX, Part 1—Psalm 114*. Wien: Musikwissenschaftlicher Verlag der Internationalen Bruckner-Gesellschaft.

Hillis, Margaret. (1991) "Anton Bruckner's *Mass in E Minor*: A Performer's Guide" in *Journal of the Conductors' Guild*, XII, No. 3 & 4 (Summer/Fall 1991), 82–95.

Kinderman, William, and Harald Krebs, eds. (1996) *The Second Practice of Nineteenth-Century Tonality*. Lincoln and London: University of Nebraska Press.

Knight, G.A.F. (1983) *Psalms*. 2 vols. Philadelphia: The Westminster Press.

Kurth, Ernst. (1971) *Bruckner*. 2 vols. Hildesheim: Georg Olms Verlag.

La Mara, ed. (1968) *Letters of Franz Liszt* (trans. Constance Bache). 2 vols. New York: Haskell House Publishers.

Maier, Elizabeth. (1988) "Der Choral in den Kirchenwerken Bruckners" in *Bruckner Symposion: Anton Bruckner und die Kirchenmusik*. Linz: Anton Bruckner Institut, Linz, 111–22.

Mayr-Kern, Josef. (1993) "Blasmusik in Oberösterreich vom 18. bis zum 20. Jahrhundert" in *Bruckner Symposion: Musikstadt Linz—Musikland Oberösterreich*. Linz: Anton Bruckner Institut, Linz, 37–46.

Nowak, Leopold, ed. (1951–91) *Anton Bruckner: Sämtliche Werke*. 32 vols. Wien: Musikwissenschaftlicher Verlag der Internationalen Bruckner-Gesellschaft.

Nowak, Leopold, ed. (1959) "*Messe E-Moll*: Fassung von 1882" in *Anton Bruckner: Sämtliche Werke*, Band 17/2. Wien: Musikwissenschaftlicher Verlag der Internationalen Bruckner-Gesellschaft.

Nowak, Leopold, ed. (1977) "*Messe E-Moll*: Fassung von 1866" in *Anton Bruckner: Sämtliche Werke*, Band 17/1. Wien: Musikwissenschaftlicher Verlag der Internationalen Bruckner-Gesellschaft.

Nowak, Leopold. (1988) "Anton Bruckner's Kirchenmusik" in *Bruckner Symposion: Anton Bruckner und die Kirchenmusik*. Linz: Anton Bruckner Institut, Linz, 85–93.

Obermayer-Mernach, Eva, ed. (1972) *Österreichisches Biographisches Lexikon 1815–1950*. Vol. V. Wien: Hermann Böhlaus Nachf.

Peters, John P. (1922) *The Psalms as Liturgies*. New York: The Macmillan Co.

Probst, Werner. (1984) "Der *Apollomarsch*—wirklich von Bruckner?" in *Österreichische Blasmusik*, No. 5/1984, 6.

Proffitt, John. (1991) Record Jacket notes for *Choral Works of Anton Bruckner*. (Albany Records CD, Troy 063).

Redlich, H. F. (1955) *Bruckner and Mahler*. London: J.M. Dent & Sons, Ltd.

Sadie, Stanley, ed. (1980) *The New Grove Dictionary of Music and Musicians*. 20 vols. London: Macmillian.

Sadie, Stanley, ed. (1988) *The Norton/Grove Concise Encyclopedia of Music*. New York: W. W. Norton & Co.

Schönzeler, Hans-Hubert. (1970) *Bruckner*. London: Calder and Boyars, Ltd.

Schulze, Willi. (1986) Preface to the score of *Anton Bruckner: Choralmesse in C—WAB 25*. Stuttgart: Carus-Verlag 40.759/01.

Simpson, Robert. (1946) "Thoughts on Bruckner's *E-Minor Mass*" in *Chord and Discord*, Vol. 2, No. 4 (1946), 30–35.

Simpson, Robert. (1967) *The Essence of Bruckner*. London: Victor Gollancz, Ltd.

Simpson, Robert. (1987) Record Jacket notes for *Bruckner: Requiem, Psalm 112, 114*. (Hyperion CD, CDA 66245).

Liber Usualis. (1952) Tornaci: Desclée & Co. (Society of St. John the Evangelist).

Suppan, Wolfgang. (1988) *Das Neue Lexicon des Blasmusikwesens*. Freiburg-Tiengen: Blasmusikverlag Schulz GmbH.

Wagner, Manfred. (1996) "Bruckner's Way to Symphony: Under the Sway of Religiosity?" in *Bruckner Special 1996*. Wien: Österreichische MUSIKZEITschrift, 17–26.

Watson, Derek. (1977) *Bruckner*. London: J. M. Dent & Sons.

Werner, Eric, Thomas H. Connolly, Paul Doe, Malcolm Boyd. (1980) "Psalm" in *New Grove Dictionary of Music and Musicians*. 20 vols., ed. by Stanley Sadie. London: Macmillan, vol. XV, 320–35.

White, Eric Walter. (1984) *Stravinsky: The Composer and His Works*. 2nd. ed. Berkeley and Los Angeles: University of California Press.

Whitwell, David. (1984) *History and Literature of the Wind Band and Wind Ensemble*. 12 vols. Northridge CA: W.I.N.D.S.

Wolff, Werner. (1973) *Anton Bruckner: Rustic Genius*. New York: Cooper Square Publishers, Inc.

Index

Adler, Guido 101
Alleluia 12, 70
Almeroth, Karl 109
Ansfelden x
Antiphon 12
Apollo-Marsch 63, 66, 131, 136
Arneth, Michael
    death 20, 23
    nameday 16, 19, 36
    prior/St. Florian xi, 1, 16, 28, 43
Assmayer, Ignaz 10, 12
Auer, Max 9, 10, 14, 16, 19, 24, 43, 51,
    63, 70, 73, 111, 113, 114, 135
Austrian *Landmesse* 2
Bach, J. S. 15, 16, 40, 51, 116, 130
Bailey, Robert 24
Bauernfeind, Hans 9
Bayer, Franz 110
Beethoven, Ludwig van 40, 130
Berlin 126
Best, Matthew 11
Braga 60
Brahms, Johannes 126, 127
Bruckner, Anton
    Abendzauber 109, 112, 113, 130,
    136
    Adagio/Symphony No. 7 127-129,
    136
    Afferentur regi 41, 43, 48, 70, 136
    Asperges me 13
    *Cantata: Auf, Brüder! auf zur fro-
    hen Feier!* 36, 136
    *Cantata: Auf, Brüder! auf, und die
    Saiten zur Hand!* 28, 45-47,

    62, 130, 136
    *Cantata: Heil, Vater! Dir zum
    hohen Feste* 16, 46, 79, 135
    *Choralmesse in C-Dur (Wind-
    haager)* 2, 5, 135
    Das deutsche Lied 118, 119, 122,
    123, 130, 136
    Das hohe Lied 104, 105, 108, 109,
    136
    "Die Nullte Symphony" 104
    Dir, Herr, dir will ich mich ergeben
    51
    E-minor Mass 13, 19, 23, 32, 41,
    47, 71, 73, 74, 82, 94, 99, 130,
    136
    Ecce sacerdos magnus 113, 114,
    118, 136
    Entsagen 16
    Festcantata: Preiset den Herrn 43,
    45, 52, 57, 62, 63, 71, 130,
    136
    Germanenzug 30, 48, 53, 54, 58,
    60, 62, 63, 85, 122, 127, 130,
    136
    Herbstlied 53
    In jener letzten der Nächte 51
    In Odin's Hallen ist es licht 53, 127
    Inveni David 66, 67, 70, 112, 136
    Jam lucis 13, 74
    Laßt Jubeltöne laut erklingen 25-
    27, 67, 136
    Libera me 20, 23, 25, 116, 130,
    135
    Litanei 133

Marsch in Es-Dur 63, 66, 130, 131, 136

Mass in D Minor 40, 41, 73, 110

Mass in F Minor 41, 73, 126

Missa ex G-moll pro Quadragesima 8, 135

Missa solemnis ix, 7, 28, 35

Os justi 13, 74

Pange lingua 13, 74

"Pausensinfonie" 102

Psalm 114 (116) 10, 11, 16, 18, 27, 130, 135

Psalm 150 104

Requiem ix, 8

Requiem/1845 67

Sängerbund 122

Stille Betrachtung an einem Herbstabend 53

String Quintet in F 67, 103, 109

"Study Symphony" 104

Symphony No. 1 65, 104

Symphony No. 2 102

Symphony No. 3 44, 103, 109

Symphony No. 4 44, 102

Symphony No. 6 67, 113

Symphony No. 7 49, 102, 103, 120, 126-129

Symphony No. 8 84, 102, 103, 113, 120

Symphony No. 9 30, 102, 118, 120-123, 125, 126

Te Deum 104, 118, 126-128

Um Mitternacht 53

Vor Arneths Grab 20, 23, 25, 130, 136

"Wagner Symphony" 103

Windhaager Mass 8

Zigeuner-Waldlied 53, 54

Zwei Aequale 8-10, 135

"a tonal anti-Christ" 103

abrupt endings 16

Alpine imagery 105, 107, 110

antiphony 21, 73, 75, 79, 80, 85-87, 91, 93, 94, 96, 107, 111, 115

assistant teacher xi, 1, 7, 102

augmented sixth chords 22, 25, 49, 58, 80, 81, 84-86, 117

bar-form 105, 110

birth x

brass chorales 51

"Bruckner rhythm" 27, 33

canon 14, 15, 30, 46, 75, 76, 79, 85, 87, 89, 90, 97

cathedral organist/Linz 26, 35, 36, 99, 113

cathedral organist/Olomouc 35

Chorale Mass 2

chorale prelude 50

chorales 9, 47, 50, 51, 85, 116

cyclic form 33, 46, 51, 52, 56, 75, 94

death 126

deputy organist/St. Florian 7

dotted rhythms 19, 45, 50, 56-58, 118-120

double tonic 24, 110

early musical education x, xi, 1, 7, 26

fermatas 9, 27, 56, 60, 76, 103, 119, 121

fugato 27, 31, 32, 42, 43, 115

fugue 15, 46, 47, 81, 82

funeral 53, 59, 126-129

"funeral music for the Master" 128

honourary doctorate 102

horn calls 30-32, 59, 60, 79, 107, 110, 112

humming choir 105, 107-112

illness 125, 126

improvisation 36, 70

"Kracher" 123

"like a watchdog that has broken his chain" 39

melodic construction 3, 18, 19, 21, 24, 26, 64, 79, 85, 106, 118

modes 13, 42, 60, 61, 74, 77, 115

modulations 2, 27, 32, 43, 47, 53, 79, 87, 112, 116

mother x, 8

Neapolitan chords 67-69, 85, 112, 116

official organist/St. Florian 7

Order of Franz Joseph 102

ostinati 79, 84, 85, 87

parallel sixth chords 14, 27, 43, 59, 75, 116

pedal points 4, 15, 24, 27, 43, 48, 59, 62, 64, 65, 70, 75, 105, 118, 121

plainchant 3, 9, 12, 30, 42, 67, 73, 77, 78, 81, 83, 95, 114, 117
polychords 23, 95
provisional organist/St. Florian 7, 8, 26
rounded binary form 64
sonata form 92
"sound cloud" 108
stylistic metamorphosis ix, 40, 41, 43, 62
third relationships 3, 9, 13, 22, 24, 27, 31, 32, 46, 48, 49, 51, 58, 59, 61, 64, 85, 106, 108, 112, 115, 119, 121
tone painting 3, 14, 15, 21, 30, 31, 49, 52, 58-62, 73, 78, 79, 82, 85-88, 90, 95, 104-107, 110-112, 120
unisons 4, 16, 19, 27, 45, 46, 51, 57, 58, 62, 67, 84, 85, 90, 95, 97, 118, 120, 122
wind works x, 8, 41, 104, 123, 130
yodellers 109-113
Bruckner, Anton Sr.
illness and death x
schoolmaster x
Bruckner, Ignaz 125
Burgstaller, Johannes 113, 115
cadenza 59, 60
Camenae 29
cantata 16, 18, 28, 33, 36, 38, 43, 53, 54
Cavalry bands 56, 63
Cecilian movement 73
Allgemeiner Deutscher Caecilien-verein 74
principles 74
Proske, K. 74
Traumihler, Ignaz 73, 74
Witt, Franz Xaver 74
Chicago Symphony Chorus 72
Cooke, Deryck 7
Corydon Singers 11
Credo I 84
Credo II 84
Credo in unum Deum 3, 84
Credo IV 84
Crown Prince Rudolf 26
Doernberg, Erwin 7, 40
Dürrnberger, August 8, 26, 35
Elizabeth

Empress of Austria 25, 26
English Chamber Orchestra 11
Enns 1
Exner, Adolf 102
falsetto 99
fauxbourdon 14, 43
Fels, Erich 118
Ferial psalm 12
First Common Mass for a Confessor Bishop 67
First Common Mass for a Virgin Martyr 42
Fourth Psalm Tone 117
Franz Joseph
Emperor of Austria 25, 26, 71, 102, 125
Fuchs, Franz 1
fugato 21, 22, 31
fugue 16, 50
Führer, Robert 35
Gabraeli, Giovanni 92
Geneva 26
German Academic Songfest 118
Gloria VIII 77
Goller, Vincenz 73
Göllerich, August 9-11, 14, 16, 19, 24, 43, 51, 63, 70, 73, 111, 113, 135
Graf, Max 131
Grasberger, Renate 113
Graz
Hochschule 118
Haas, Robert 65
Händel, G. F.
Halleluia 70
Hanslick, Eduard 103, 104
Harrandt, Dr. Andrea 128
Hawkshaw, Paul 11, 17, 37, 40-42, 60
Hellmesberger, Joseph 103
Herbeck, Johann von 39, 101
Libera 126
Hillis, Margaret 72
Hörsching x
Immaculate Conception 43, 48, 49, 51
Infantry bands 63
Internationale Bruckner-Gesellschaft 128
Jobst, Maria 2
Kalliwoda, Johann Wenzel 123
Das deutsche Lied 122

Kattinger, Anton 7
Keldorfer, Viktor 110, 112, 113
Kéler, Béla 63
    Mazzuchelli March, op. 22 131
Kitzler, Otto 39-41, 44, 45, 52, 53, 63,
131
Kitzler Studienbuch 40
Klose, Friedrich 102
Kränzl, Joseph 54
Kremsmünster 7, 17, 41, 42
Kronstorf 1
Kurth, Ernst 72, 73
Kyrie Deus sempiterne 2
Landini cadence 31
Lanz, Engelbert 44
    Misit Dominus 44
Leipzig 102, 127
Lesser Doxology 114, 117
Levi, Hermann 103
Liadov, Anatole
    The Enchanted Lake, op. 62 113
Liber Usualis 11, 12
Liedertafel Frohsinn 25, 26, 36, 44, 53,
    54, 66, 67, 71
Linz x, 11, 25, 26, 35, 36, 40, 41, 43,
    53, 63, 71, 72, 91, 101, 114,
    122, 133
    Austro-Hungarian Infantry Regi-
        ment No. 14 band 71
    centennial of diocese 72, 113
    Hessen Regiment band 56, 63
    Jäger-Truppe band 63, 131
    Linzer Zeitung 53
    Municipal Theatre 39
    Musikverein 71
    New cathedral 43, 49, 71, 72, 113
    Old cathedral 72
    Pfarrkirche 36
    Sängerbund 71
    Votive Chapel/'New' cathedral
        71-73
Liszt, Franz 39, 41, 73, 103
London 102
Löwe, Ferdinand 102, 127-129
Mader, Raoul 118
Maecenas, Gaius Cilnius 29
Mahler, Gustav 102
Maier, Elizabeth 2
Männergesang-Vereinen 44
Marinelli, Ernst

canon/St. Florian 17, 23, 29, 37
Mattig, Heinrich von der 104, 105, 109
Mayr, Friedrich
    nameday 17, 28, 37
    prior/St. Florian 17, 28, 35, 43
Mayrhofer, Rosalie 8
Mazzuchelli, Alois Count 131
Mendelssohn, Felix 19, 21, 33, 40
    Cantata: Lobgesang 45, 51
    St. Paul 40
    Symphony No. 2 45, 47, 50
    influence on Bruckner 40
mezza voce 99
Michaelmas Day 71
missa brevis 2
Mottl, Felix 101, 128
Mozart, W. A. 16, 21
    Requiem 21
Munich 93
Nancy 102
Neubauer, Josef 105, 127
"New German School" 103
Nikisch, Arthur 101, 127, 128
Nowak, Leopold 3, 7, 72, 99
Nürnburg 66
Oberösterreichisches Sängerfest 53
Oberösterreichisches-Salzburgisches
    Sängerbundesfest 54, 122
Olomouc 35
organum 114, 115
Palestrina, G. P. da 73, 74, 85, 91, 99,
    130
    Missa brevis 89
Pamesberger, Prof. Dr. 44, 48
Paris 102
Paschal time 12
Paur, Emil 101
Perger, Richard von 126, 127
Phrygian cadence 61
Polzer, Prof. Aurelius 118
Pope Pius IX 43
Prague 35
Primiz 17
Probst, Werner 131
Psalm 114 11, 12
Psalm 115 11
Psalm 116 11
Psalm 45 42
Psalm 88 67
Richter, Hans 129

Rietsch, Heinrich 131
ritornello 114, 115, 117, 118
Rochberg, George ix
Rott, Hans 102
Rudigier, Franz Joseph
    bishop/Linz 36, 43, 71, 101
Salzburg 118, 123
Schalk, Franz 102, 128
Schalk, Joseph 102, 120, 128
Schiedermayer
    dean/Linz cathedral 72
Schimatschek, Franz 63
Schönberg, Arnold
    Summer Morning by the Lake, op.
        16, No. 3 113
Schreyer, Adalbert 91
Schubert, Franz 130
    Am Tage Allerseelen 126
Sechter, Simon 35-37, 39-41, 43, 101,
        133
senza misura 61
Silberstein, August 53-55, 59
Simpson, Robert 16, 36, 77, 96
Solemn Reception of a Bishop 114
Solgofnir 60, 61
St. Antoninus 67
St. Florian xi, 1, 7, 8, 10, 12, 20, 23, 26,
        28, 35-37, 41-43, 73, 101,
        127, 130
St. Lucy 42
Steyr 1, 109, 110, 125
    Stadtpfarrkirche 110, 130
Strauss, Johann 126
Stravinsky, I.
    Octuor 72
stretto 16, 82
United States of America 102
Valhalla 59, 62
Valkyrie 59, 61
Venetian school 75
Venice 128
versicle-response 30, 73
Vespers 12
Vienna 10, 25, 26, 71, 101, 102
    Academic Choral Society 53, 104,
        118, 127
    Augustinian church 25
    Austrian National Library 63, 128
    Belvedere Palace 125-127
    Conservatory 39, 101-103, 126

Court Opera 39, 53, 127
Deutsche Zeitung 127
Gesellschaft der Musikfreunde 39,
    126, 127
Hofkapelle 101
Hofopernorchester 129
Karlskirche 126, 127, 129
Kustodenstöckl 125
Männergesang-Verein 39, 110,
    113, 126
musical press 103, 126
Philharmonic 39, 102, 103, 129
Piaristenkirche 39
Stephansdom 130
teacher-training college, St. Anna
    101
Tenth Austrian Infantry Regiment
    131
Universal Edition 73, 129
University 101, 102
Wagner tubas 127-129
Wagner, Hans 104, 105
Wagner, Manfred 3, 4
Wagner, Richard 16, 103, 128
    Der Ring des Nibelungen 55, 110
    Die Meistersinger 66, 67, 69
    Die Walküre 51
    Parsifal 3
    Tannhäuser 40, 41, 57
    Tristan 24, 93
    death 103, 127, 128
    influence on Bruckner 40, 41, 53,
        69, 128
    Rheinmaidens 110
Wallmann, Dr. Heinrich 104
Weilnböck, Karl 49
Weingartner, Felix 120
Weinwurm, Rudolf 54, 60, 71, 101
    Germania 54
Weiss, Johann Baptist x
    Requiem in E-flat x
Whitsun 12, 118
Windhaag 1, 2, 102
Wolf, Hugo 102, 126
    Die Feuerreiter 126
    Elfenlied 126
Women's Choral Society of Vöcklabruck
    114
Wöss, Josef V. 129

About the Author

KEITH WILLIAM KINDER is an Associate Professor of music at McMaster University, Hamilton-Ontario. He received his doctoral degree in instrumental conducting from the University of Colorado.

ISBN 0-313-30834-9

90000>

HARDCOVER BAR CODE